ECHOES of GLORY

TIME ®
LIFE
BOOKS

Time-Life Books also publishes a series of books that chronicles in full the events of the American Civil War, 1861-1865. The titles are:

BROTHER AGAINST BROTHER *The War Begins*
FIRST BLOOD *Fort Sumter to Bull Run*
THE BLOCKADE *Runners and Raiders*
THE ROAD TO SHILOH *Early Battles in the West*
FORWARD TO RICHMOND *McClellan's Peninsular Campaign*
DECOYING THE YANKS *Jackson's Valley Campaign*
CONFEDERATE ORDEAL *The Southern Home Front*
LEE TAKES COMMAND *From Seven Days to Second Bull Run*
THE COASTAL WAR *Chesapeake Bay to Rio Grande*
TENTING TONIGHT *The Soldier's Life*
THE BLOODIEST DAY *The Battle of Antietam*
WAR ON THE MISSISSIPPI *Grant's Vicksburg Campaign*
REBELS RESURGENT *Fredericksburg to Chancellorsville*
TWENTY MILLION YANKEES *The Northern Home Front*
GETTYSBURG *The Confederate High Tide*
THE STRUGGLE FOR TENNESSEE *Tupelo to Stones River*
THE FIGHT FOR CHATTANOOGA *Chickamauga to Missionary Ridge*
SPIES, SCOUTS AND RAIDERS *Irregular Operations*
THE BATTLES FOR ATLANTA *Sherman Moves East*
THE KILLING GROUND *Wilderness to Cold Harbor*
SHERMAN'S MARCH *Atlanta to the Sea*
DEATH IN THE TRENCHES *Grant at Petersburg*
WAR ON THE FRONTIER *The Trans-Mississippi West*
THE SHENANDOAH IN FLAMES *The Valley Campaign of 1864*
PURSUIT TO APPOMATTOX *The Last Battles*
THE ASSASSINATION *The Death of the President*
THE NATION REUNITED *War's Aftermath*
MASTER INDEX *An Illustrated Guide*

For information on and a full description of the Time-Life
Books series listed above, please call 1-800-621-7026 or write:
Reader Information
Time-Life Customer Service
P.O. Box 85568
Richmond, Virginia 23285-5568

Echoes of Glory is a three-volume set. The other titles are:

Arms and Equipment of the Confederacy
Arms and Equipment of the Union

The Cover: This photograph taken on Stafford Heights
shows the gunners of Captain Franklin A. Pratt's Battery M,
1st Connecticut Heavy Artillery, as they prepared Confederate
positions across the Rappahannock below Fredericksburg.
The battery was armed with 4.5-inch rifled siege guns.

Credit: William Gladstone Collection, USAMHI, copies by
A. Pierce Bounds.

Cover design by Redruth, Robin Bray, Proprietor.

ECHOES of GLORY

Civil War

Battle Atlas

By the Editors of Time-Life Books

TIME-LIFE BOOKS · ALEXANDRIA · VIRGINIA

Time-Life Books is a division of Time Life Inc.

TIME LIFE INC.
PRESIDENT and CEO: George Artandi

TIME-LIFE BOOKS
PRESIDENT: John D. Hall
PUBLISHER/MANAGING EDITOR: Neil Kagan
Vice President, Director of Finance: Christopher
  Hearing
Vice President, Book Production: Marjann Caldwell
Director of Operations: Eileen Bradley
Director of Photography and Research: John Conrad
  Weiser
Director of Editorial Administration: Barbara Levitt
Chief Librarian: Louise D. Forstall

ECHOES OF GLORY
Editor: Henry Woodhead
Administrator: Jane Edwin
Art Directors: Dale Pollekoff, Herbert H. Quarmby
Deputy Editors: Harris J. Andrews, Kirk E. Denkler

Editorial Staff for *Illustrated Atlas of the Civil War*
Writer: Maggie Debelius
Associate Editor/Research: Quentin Gaines Story
Senior Copy Coordinator: Anne Farr
Picture Coordinator: Gail V. Feinberg
Research Assistant/Maps: Jayne A. L. Dover
Production Manager: Prudence G. Harris
Quality Assurance Manager: James King

Special Contributors: Margery A. duMond, Stephen G.
Hyslop, M. Linda Lee, Brian C. Pohanka, David S.
Thomson (text); Anthony K. Pordes, Carolee B.
Walker (copy); Adam Cornelius (maps); Anne K.
DuVivier (art); Roy Nanovic (index).

Correspondents: Elisabeth Kraemer-Singh (Bonn),
Christine Hinze (London), Christina Lieberman (New
York), Maria Vincenza Aloisi (Paris), Ann Natanson
(Rome).

Consultant:

Col. John R. Elting, USA (Ret.), former associate professor
at West Point, has written or edited some 20 books,
including *Swords around a Throne, The Superstrategists,*
and *American Army Life,* as well as *Battles for Scandi-
navia* in the Time-Life Books World War II series. He was
chief consultant to the Time-Life series The Civil War.

Printed in 1996. © MCMXCI Time-Life Books.
Second printing. Printed in U.S.A.
Originally published as *Illustrated Atlas of the Civil War.*

Library of Congress Cataloging in Publication Data
Illustrated atlas of the Civil War / by the editors of
  Time-Life Books.
      p.   cm. — (Echoes of glory)
  Includes bibliographical references and index.
  ISBN: 0-7835-4892-3
    ISBN 0-8094-8858-2 (trade)
    ISBN 0-8094-8859-0 (lib. bdg.)
    1. United States—History—Civil War, 1861-1865—
Campaigns—Maps.
    2. United States—History—Civil War, 1861-1865—
Battlefields—Maps.
    I. Time-Life Books. II. Series.
    G1201.S514 1991 (G&M)
    973.7'3'0223—dc20   91-8727 CIP   MAP

Contents

INTRODUCTION 6

EASTERN THEATER 20

FIRST BULL RUN/FIRST MANASSAS 24

1862 VALLEY CAMPAIGN 34

PENINSULAR CAMPAIGN 44

SECOND BULL RUN CAMPAIGN 56

ANTIETAM CAMPAIGN 68

FREDERICKSBURG 86

CHANCELLORSVILLE 98

GETTYSBURG CAMPAIGN 110

WILDERNESS CAMPAIGN 134

1864 VALLEY CAMPAIGN 152

PETERSBURG TO APPOMATTOX 166

WESTERN THEATER 190

SHILOH 194

1862 KENTUCKY/TENNESSEE CAMPAIGN 206

MISSISSIPPI RIVER CAMPAIGN 216

CHATTANOOGA CAMPAIGN 232

ATLANTA CAMPAIGN 248

1864 TENNESSEE CAMPAIGN 270

SHERMAN'S MARCH 280

COASTAL WAR 286

ATLANTIC COAST 288

MOBILE BAY 298

FORT FISHER 300

FAR WEST 302

MISSOURI/ARKANSAS CAMPAIGN 304

NEW MEXICO CAMPAIGN 308

RED RIVER CAMPAIGN 310

ACKNOWLEDGMENTS 314

PICTURE CREDITS 314

BIBLIOGRAPHY 316

INDEX 317

The Trials of Command

The Civil War was less than four months old, but the soldiers of the 79th New York reckoned they had already seen enough fighting to last a lifetime. Like many of the Northern and Southern volunteers who answered the call to arms in April 1861, these New Yorkers had mustered around the nucleus of a pre-War militia unit, the Highland Guard, one of Manhattan's most colorful military organizations. Its 300 members sported full Scottish regalia, including rakish glengarry caps, kilts, and checkered stockings. When the Highlanders marched off to war on June 2, they mustered a full 10 companies, their ranks having been swelled by nearly 600 recruits eager to take part in the great battle most thought would bring a quick end to the fledgling Southern Confederacy.

That battle came near a Virginia stream called Bull Run on July 21, 1861. It was a brutal introduction to combat for the 79th New York and other hastily recruited volunteer regiments. The Highlanders lost 198 men killed, wounded, or missing, 11 of them officers. Colonel James Cameron, the regimental commander and brother of United States Secretary of War Simon Cameron, was among the slain. Swept away in the rout of Brigadier General Irvin McDowell's Federal forces, the survivors of the 79th New York straggled back to the safety of Washington. Surveying his chastened comrades, Private William Todd thought that " 'I want to go home' was pictured on every countenance."

After 17 officers signed a petition asking that the regiment be allowed to return to New York to "reorganize," Secretary of War Cameron indicated he would endorse the request. Lieutenant Colonel Samuel Elliott, now in charge, told his men to prepare for the trip. But instead of a furlough, on August 10 the Highlanders received a new colonel.

Isaac Ingalls Stevens stood only an inch over five feet; but the swarthy little colonel exhibited a stern determination that belied his diminutive stature. After graduating first in the class of 1839 at West Point, Stevens had served with distinction as a military engineer in the Mexican War before leaving the army to seek his fortune on the western frontier. He had led several surveying expeditions, fought Indians, and pursued a political career as the governor of the Washington Territory and territorial delegate to Congress. Hot-tempered, ambitious, and profane, Stevens had a penchant for controversy; his sympathy for proslavery Democrats at first made it difficult for him to obtain a command in the Federal forces. Stevens was "strong in his likes and dislikes," one associate recalled, "but the very best organizer and disciplinarian that I ever met." Major General George B. McClellan, who had assumed command of the army at Washington in the wake of the disaster at Bull Run, believed Stevens' skills could be put to good use in shaping up the battered 79th New York.

Isaac Stevens had no intention of allowing his homesick volunteers to take a holiday from the grim realities of war. For their part, the men in the ranks considered Stevens' appointment "a piece of high-handed interference on the part of the government"; in accordance with standard militia procedure, they had wanted to elect their new commander. All but 10 subordinate officers promptly resigned, dozens of enlisted men sought to drown their troubles in cheap whiskey, and on August 14, when Colonel Stevens ordered his unit to fall in and march to a new campsite, the troops refused to budge.

When word of the apparent mutiny reached McClellan, he dispatched Regular Army troops with artillery to surround the Highlanders' camp at Meridian Hill on the outskirts of Washington. As the regulars filed into line around the muttering New Yorkers, Stevens again called his men to attention. "You are soldiers, and your duty is to obey," he barked. "I am your colonel, and your obedience is due to me." If they refused to fall into line, they would be fired upon. The Highlanders grudgingly obliged, whereupon the ringleaders of the mutiny were called out of formation, put in irons, and led away to a military prison. Stevens told Lieutenant Colonel Elliott he had half an hour in which to resign or face a court-martial. Elliott resigned.

An order from McClellan was read, depriving the 79th New York of its colors. The flags would not be returned to the Highlanders until they "learned the first duty of soldiers—obedience—and have proven on the field of battle that they are not wanting in courage." An observer recalled when the colorbearers surrendered their banners, "a low cry like a protesting moan" rose from the assembled ranks. The cowed New Yorkers marched to their new encampment, cherishing a bitter hatred and a healthy respect for their commander.

At "Camp Hope," Colonel Stevens set about the task of transforming his malcontents into military men. There were predawn roll calls, constant drills, and an unrelenting insistence on Regular Army standards of dress and deportment. Men who refused to wash regularly were marched to the Potomac River under guard, stripped, and scrubbed with brooms. At the same time, Stevens made sure that good conduct was rewarded with promotion and leaves of absence. Most important, Stevens saw to it that after his unit performed well in a skirmish with Confederate forces near Lewinsville, Virginia, the precious regimental colors were returned. General McClellan made the presentation in person, telling the men they "had acquitted themselves as true soldiers."

So completely had Isaac Stevens won over the recalcitrant New Yorkers that when he was promoted to brigadier general the men of the 79th insisted on

Considered an officer of great promise, Isaac I. Stevens adroitly restored order to the mutinous 79th New York Highlanders after he was appointed their colonel in August 1861. Promoted to brigadier and later major general, he distinguished himself in the South Carolina coastal campaign and commanded a division at Second Bull Run.

being transferred to his new command. The noncommissioned officers and privates raised funds for an ornate sword, sash, and spurs, which they presented to Stevens with "a unanimous feeling of gratitude and respect for our colonel, our friend, and our counselor," who had rescued the regiment "from the vortex of anarchy."

At the height of the Battle of Chantilly, Virginia, on September 1, 1862, Isaac Stevens again took the flag of the 79th New York, this time to lead the embattled unit in a charge on Stonewall Jackson's Confederates. Stevens was shouting "Highlanders, my Highlanders, follow your general!" when he was killed instantly by a bullet through the head. The regiment's surivors later sent the ripped and bloodstained banner to Stevens' widow, along with a note that read, "His memory is engraven on the hearts of every one of his Highlanders."

One of Napoleon's military maxims was that "in war, moral considerations make up three-quarters of the game." In Isaac Stevens, the 79th New York had been fortunate to find a commander who possessed those qualities of leadership that infused a command—be it a company or an army—with the esprit de corps so necessary to success in war.

The quality of leadership was crucial to the outcome of the battles and campaigns detailed in this volume. From Bull Run to Appomattox Courthouse, the tactics and strategies that came to be symbolized on the battle maps of the War evolved in the minds of men whose abilities ranged from stellar to abysmal. Both armies possessed, in full measure, their share of excellent and poor leaders, and those in between. From the lieutenants to the generals, the men who led troops in the Civil War came in every variety: the brilliant and the dull-witted, the reckless and the cautious, the pious and the profane.

While the Civil War saw both armies take advantage of technological advances in weaponry and communications—the railroad and the telegraph —the art of generalship had changed little in a hundred years. Generals were expected not only to plan, to administer, to organize, to oversee; they were frequently called upon to lead their men in a literal sense. At times, as in the case of Stevens, they paid for it with their lives: 47 Federal and 77 Confederate generals were either killed or mortally wounded in the forefront of attack.

Heroics on the part of senior officers, however, were no guarantee of success on the battlefield. Virginia cavalryman Frank Myers judged his swashbuckling brigade commander, Brigadier General Thomas L. Rosser, to be "as brave a man as ever drew breath"; but, Myers noted, "he knows no more about putting a command into a fight than a schoolboy." At the Battle of Antietam, Federal Major General Edwin V. Sumner, commander of II Corps, personally led one of his divisions in an assault, but left the commanders of his remaining two divisions with only the vaguest idea of what they were supposed to do. The resulting attacks were disjointed and less than successful.

"No great mental powers are needed to maneuver a brigade of infantry," claimed Federal Brigadier General Francis Barlow. "The difficulty of the problem increases as the numbers increase, and therefore it happens that many a man can handle a brigade admirably, who can do nothing with a corps or even a division." Just as the regimental commander had to master the intricacies of battalion drill, so the brigade or division commander had to familiarize himself with the geometrical choreography involved in maneuvering larger bodies of troops. "School teaching is at best a laborious business," wrote John Gibbon, who was appointed to lead a brigade of Union infantry after serving 14 years in the Regular Army artillery. "But when the scholars number several thousand and the head teacher has as assistants but few who know even the ABC of the subject to be taught, the task becomes Herculean." Gibbon found his artillery experience of limited value in deploying four regiments of infantry. Like many of his volunteer officers, Gibbon often resorted to consulting the drill manual before giving his commands.

Perhaps the most common cause of mistakes on the battlefield was poor staff work. A general's staff was his military family, and could vary in number from six or eight officers for a brigade commander up to as many as two dozen or more for an army commander. Their duties were many, and often of an administrative nature. Depending upon the size of the organization, there were commissaries to oversee the distribution of food, quartermasters to deal with supply, a medical director to coordinate the ambulance trains and field hospitals, as well as adjutants who kept track of the daily troop strength through reports required of every regimental commander.

Once the battle was joined, a commander communicated with his officers in the field through his staff. Not only orderlies and aides-de-camp, but frequently administrative personnel were called upon to carry orders—written or oral—to implement the wishes of their superior. But in battles in which the fronts of the opposing armies often measured more than five miles, generals habitually found their overworked staffs inadequate for the task at hand. "Scarcely any of our generals had what they needed to keep a constant and close supervision on the execution of important orders," recalled the Confederate artillerist Porter Alexander. "An army is like a great machine, and putting it into battle it is not enough for its commander to merely issue the necessary orders. He should have a staff ample to supervise the execution of each step and to promptly report any difficulty or misunderstanding."

Despite the flaws found in Northern and Southern armies, one of the irrefutable facts of the Civil War was the superiority of Confederate military leadership during the first two years of the conflict. There were many reasons for the strength of the Southern officer corps. Jefferson Davis, the Confederate president, was an 1828 graduate of West Point, had served with distinction as colonel of Mississippi volunteers in the Mexican War, and had held the post of secretary of war in the administration of Franklin Pierce. Unlike Lincoln—whose only military experience had consisted of a three-month stint in the Illinois militia during the Black Hawk War—Davis rarely permitted politics to dictate his selection of military commanders.

"An army is like a great machine, and putting it into battle it is not enough for its commander to merely issue the necessary orders. He should have a staff ample to supervise the execution of each step."

COL. E. PORTER ALEXANDER
ARTILLERY COMMANDER
LONGSTREET'S CORPS
ARMY OF NORTHERN VIRGINIA

12

General Robert E. Lee, astride his gray mount Traveller, pauses under an oak tree with his senior officers to reconnoiter an enemy position. The artist took creative license with this painting by including several prominent generals who never served in Lee's Army of Northern Virginia.

The Confederacy, in addition, possessed a wealth of homegrown military talent. Although a majority of West Pointers stood by the Union, many of the military academy's most distinguished alumni resigned from the Regular Army to cast their lot with the Confederacy. The prewar South had an established military tradition that made the pursuit of an army career far more attractive there than in the North. Schools such as the Virginia Military Institute and the South Carolina Military Academy provided the Confederacy with some two dozen generals and scores of talented regimental and staff officers. The Army of Northern Virginia alone counted 167 field-grade officers who had graduated from Southern military institutions. In the South, moreover, there was a sense of great urgency about choosing military leaders; the fledgling nation faced an immediate threat to its survival that made the recognition of military talent of vital importance.

The Federal army, conversely, was to some extent saddled with the existing military structure—a hierarchy founded upon seniority rather than ability. Federal Brigadier General Alpheus Williams referred to it as "the cursed policy of old fogyism." Those tough, dashing officers who had made names for themselves in earlier wars, and who aroused great expectations, had grown old and stiff in staff or garrison duties. Moreover, political patronage was a fact of life for the Lincoln administration, and the price for the cooperation of the Northern "war governors" was often the promotion of a political crony to a rank he was not qualified to hold.

Federal commanders often seemed to be working at cross-purposes rather than employing the cohesive strategy that Winfield Scott had envisioned. Even before the first battles were fought, Scott—the physically infirm but mentally acute septuagenarian who had served for 30 years as general-in-chief of the U.S. Army—determined that the War was likely to be a drawn-out and bloody affair. Victory would be attained only if the Union could make full use of its marked superiority in industry, transport, and manpower.

Scott proposed a naval blockade of Southern coastal ports, together with the seizure of the Mississippi River from the mouth of the Ohio to the Gulf of Mexico. Union occupation of these vital arteries of supply would slowly but inexorably strangle the Confederacy into submission.

Northern firebrands who cherished delusions of a quick and easy victory over the rebellious states scoffed at Scott's so-called Anaconda Plan, named for the huge South American snake that slowly crushes its prey to death. Scott would soon step aside so that younger men might take up the challenges of command. But his plan provided the framework for the successful coordination of Northern forces that ultimately vanquished the Southern Confederacy.

At the beginning of the War, however, coordination seemed an unattainable goal. In 1862, Stonewall Jackson was able to defeat four separate Federal contingents in the Shenandoah Valley despite odds that were four to one in his opponents' favor. Jackson's rapid marches and superior strategy played a part

Major Thomas Jonathan Jackson, later to be known as Stonewall *(above),* joined the faculty of the Virginia Military Institute in 1851 to teach science and artillery tactics—a career he was still pursuing six years later when this picture was taken. Although destined for greatness, Jackson as a teacher was a droning pedagogue and an object of ridicule known to his students as Fool Tom.

William Oates. Lee maintained a close and deferential working relationship with Jefferson Davis, and gained his support when he set about reorganizing his forces and reshuffling his army's command structure in the wake of the Seven Days' Battles in the summer of 1862.

There was more to Lee, however, than his dignified image and administrative skills. He was a consummate campaigner, a skilled tactician, and a daring strategist. He was willing to risk defeat to attain victory. "He never allowed his adversary quietly to mature and carry out his own plan of campaign," an artilleryman recalled. "Although conducting a defensive struggle, he was yet generally the attacking party." Lee's willingness to divide his forces in the face of a numerically superior foe, then to fall on his enemy's flank or rear, as he did in the Second Manassas campaign and at Chancellorsville, prompted the Confed-

Abraham Lincoln confers privately with General George B. McClellan inside the general's tent at Sharpsburg, Maryland, in early October 1862, following the Battle of Antietam. On the ground at lower left is a Confederate battle flag taken during the Maryland campaign. In early November, Lincoln relieved McClellan of command of the Army of the Potomac for his failure to pursue the Confederates.

in his triumph, but so did the utter lack of cooperation among the Union commanders. Indeed, many of the Union's officers appeared to be more interested in personal glory than in a shared victory. "Officers are more selfish, dishonest, and grasping in their struggle for notoriety than the miser for gold," Colonel John Beatty complained.

Repeated failures spurred Abraham Lincoln's frustrating quest for generals who would vigorously prosecute the War. When Major General Don Carlos Buell failed to exploit strategically his tactical victory at Perryville, Kentucky, in October 1862, Lincoln said he could not comprehend why the Northern forces seemed unable to "march as the enemy marches, live as he lives, and fight as he fights, unless we admit the inferiority of our troops and of our generals."

Ironically, the administration's penchant for allowing political expediency to override military necessity was itself a prime cause of Union failure on the battlefield. Until the last year of the War, politically influential but militarily inept commanders like Benjamin F. Butler, Nathaniel P. Banks, and Franz Sigel were entrusted with the command of armies in the field. It was a situation that fostered a cynical pessimism among many subordinate Federal officers.

David A. Russell, commander of a division in VI Corps, Army of the Potomac, concluded that the Union army had become "about as much a political machine as any other branch or department of our government." In a letter to his family, Captain William Lusk declared that "the whole batch of our political generals are objects of honest terror to every soldier in the Union army." Some officers were outspoken in their condemnation of what they considered the deplorable inefficiency of the authorities in Washington. "Was there ever such a government, such fools, such idiots?" Lieutenant Colonel Alexander Webb wrote his father after the Union defeat at Second Bull Run in August 1862. "I hate and despise them more intensely than I do the Rebels."

> *"The whole batch of our political generals are objects of honest terror to every soldier in the Union army."*
>
> CAPT. WILLIAM LUSK
> 79TH NEW YORK INFANTRY REGIMENT
> ARMY OF THE POTOMAC

Webb was no churlish malcontent. Educated at West Point, he became a general at 28, was twice wounded, and received the Congressional Medal of Honor for his gallantry at Gettysburg. His views were shared by many of the young officers who rose to prominence in the Federal service. Undoubtedly one aspect of Webb's frustration was that the force in which he served—the Army of the Potomac—was the best trained, armed, and equipped but least successful of the major Federal armies. It failed mainly because it suffered from a series of flawed commanders, but also because its principal foe, the Army of Northern Virginia, was led by the greatest of all Confederate generals: Robert E. Lee.

The most highly regarded officer of the U.S. Army to join the Confederacy, Lee embodied innate dignity, aristocratic reserve, and quiet determination that elicited almost instinctive respect from his subordinates. "The fear of incurring his displeasure at all times enforced implicit obedience," wrote Colonel erate cavalry officer William P. Roberts to call him "the greatest general the world has produced, Napoleon not excepted."

Lee's soldiers regarded him with a devotion that bordered on reverence. General Porter Alexander described the "wave of sentiment" that swept through the ranks at an 1864 review of the artillery of Longstreet's corps. "Each man seemed to feel the bond which held us all to Lee," Alexander wrote. "The effect was that of a military sacrament, in which we pledged anew our lives." When a Confederate chaplain asked one of Lee's aides, "Does it not make the General proud to see how these men love him?" the officer replied, "Not proud, it awes him."

The Virginia artillery officer Robert Stiles recognized the military strength inspired by the symbiotic connection between Lee and his army, an alliance "constant and permanent, undissolved and indissoluble." What was more, Stiles and his Confederate comrades recognized a difference between Lee and his counterparts in the Union camp. "We came to look with wonder, not unmixed with pity, upon the contrasted condition of the opposing Federal army, with generals jealous of and plotting against one another, and the government forever pulling down one and putting up another."

Lee's principal antagonist in the first two years of the War was Major General George Brinton McClellan, a man whose undenied organizational skills transformed the Army of the Potomac into a well-drilled military machine and whose youthful energy seemed to presage great deeds on the field of battle. The newspapers dubbed him the Young Napoleon, and the bond he forged with his men elicited a devotion not unlike that which the Army of Northern Virginia felt for Lee. While enforcing discipline, McClellan nonetheless was careful to maintain a rapport with the enlisted men. One officer thought "his bow and smile seemed to carry a little of personal good fellowship even to the humblest private soldier." The brigade commander Alexander Hays declared that the excitement McClellan generated as he rode along the lines of cheering troops "amounted to wildness."

Unlike Lee, however, McClellan proved consistently unable to make decisive use of his army's potential, nor was he able to maintain an amicable working relationship with the Lincoln administration. "The realities of war seemed to daze him," General Joshua Chamberlain recalled. "With all that marvelous magnetism which won the love and enthusiasm of his subordinates, he lacked the skill, or the will, to gain the sympathy of his superiors."

In fact, what General McClellan lacked most of all was that Napoleonic virtue that Confederate Robert E. Lee possessed in abundance: the willingness to take risks. "I feel that the salvation of the country demands the utmost prudence on my part," McClellan wrote. "I must not run the slightest risk of disaster." He believed "the one safe rule in war" was "to decide what is the very worst thing that can happen to you and prepare to meet it." The Union general professed to seek "bloodless victories," as he abhorred "the sickening sight of the battlefield, with its mangled corpses and poor suffering wounded."

McClellan's inability to take Richmond in the summer of 1862, after having brought his forces to within six miles of the Confederate capital, his yielding of the initiative to his opponents in the Seven Days' Battles, and most of all his failure to destroy Lee's army in the wake of the strategic Federal victory at Antietam ultimately cost the Young Napoleon his command. But in light of other generals' even more costly reverses—Ambrose Burnside's repulse at Fredericksburg and Joseph Hooker's defeat at Chancellorsville—McClellan's name continued to hold a certain magic for his old soldiers. "Give us back McClellan and we will fight again," one New Yorker wrote after the slaughter at Fredericksburg, "feeling certain that we shall not be led to certain death without accomplishing anything." As late as the summer of 1864, Captain Oliver Wendell Holmes, Jr., told his family, "There's no use in disguising that the feeling for McClellan has grown."

Even the most successful commander of the Army of the Potomac, Major General George G. Meade, fell prey to a McClellan-like inertia after the Union victory at Gettysburg. "It was a grand battle," Meade informed his wife, "and is in my judgment a most decided victory, though I did not annihilate or bag the Confederate army." Rather than risk a bloody repulse, Meade allowed Robert E. Lee's forces to complete their withdrawal across the Potomac River. When Lincoln expressed his displeasure at the lost opportunity, Meade reported that his troops were exhausted and needed "rest and reorganization." To Meade's way of thinking, "The proper policy for the Government would have been to be contented with driving Lee out of Maryland."

Most of the early Federal leaders in the War's Western theater shared McClellan's shortcomings. The army commanders Don Carlos Buell, Henry Halleck, and William S. Rosecrans all proved unwilling or unable to exploit a strategic advantage. It was perhaps fortunate for the Union cause that for a crucial year and a half the Confederacy's most important Western force—the Army of Tennessee—was entrusted to Braxton Bragg.

"This officer is in appearance the least prepossessing of the Confederate generals," wrote the British observer Arthur Fremantle. "He stoops, and has a sickly, cadaverous, haggard appearance." Bragg had a distinguished record as a battery commander in the Mexican War, where he had struck up a friendship with then-Colonel Jefferson Davis. He was hardworking and a good organizer; but he was also dour, irascible, and quirky.

Although he had once asserted that victory was "never complete until every enemy is killed, wounded, or captured," Bragg chose to abandon his invasion of Kentucky after a hard-fought battle with Buell's Army of the Ohio at Perryville. Three months later, on January 3, 1863, Bragg again withdrew, this time after being turned back by Rosecrans' troops at Stones River in Tennessee. In September 1863, Bragg failed to pursue Rosecrans' retreating forces from the battlefield of Chickamauga. Had he done so, Bragg might well have been

Ironically, Major General Braxton Bragg *(above)*, an officer generally despised by the rank and file of the Confederate army for his flawed leadership, once paid an eloquent tribute to the common soldier. "We have had to trust to the individuality and self-reliance of the private soldier," he wrote after the Battle of Stones River during the winter of 1862-1863. "Without the incentive which controls the officer; without the hope of reward, and actuated only by a sense of duty and of patriotism, he has, in this great contest, justly judged that the cause was his own and gone into it with a determination to conquer or die."

able to deal the North a severe setback by finishing off Rosecrans' army.

Unlike the courtly and tactful Lee, Bragg was unable to mollify his often quarrelsome subordinates, many of whom bore an ill-concealed contempt for their commander. When General Nathan Bedford Forrest took exception to one of Bragg's orders, the fiery cavalryman told his superior, "You have played the part of a damned scoundrel and are a coward; if you ever again try to interfere with me or cross my path it will be at the peril of your life." In October of 1863, a dozen of the Army of Tennessee's senior generals addressed a petition to President Davis requesting Bragg's replacement.

Bragg was just as unpopular with the men in the ranks. "He loved to crush the spirit of his men," declared the Tennessee private Sam Watkins. "Not a single soldier in the whole army ever loved or respected him." Bragg's humiliating defeat in the November 1863 Battle of Chattanooga finally brought about his transfer, but he left the army in a state one soldier described as a "sullen, dangerous demoralization."

Bragg's military demise coincided with the emergence of Ulysses S. Grant as the preeminent Federal leader. Grant's early victories at Forts Henry and Donelson had secured the Tennessee River for the Union, and he had demonstrated a remarkable capacity for tactical skill during the campaign that culminated in the surrender of the Confederate stronghold of Vicksburg, Mississippi. His defeat of Bragg at Chattanooga was one of the War's turning points.

Though singularly colorless by standards of martial bearing, the unostentatious general had the aggressive instinct so many Federal commanders lacked. "Grant is not a very fine looking general," a Federal colonel wrote, "but he has the appearance of a man of determination." Lieutenant Colonel Theodore Lyman told his wife that Grant "habitually wears an expression as if he had determined to drive his head through a brick wall, and was about to do it."

By early 1864, the Confederacy had lost more than 100,000 square miles of territory, had relinquished the transportation lifeline of the Mississippi River, and was slowly starving from the effects of the Federal naval blockade. Troop morale was eroding, and irreplaceable losses were crippling the offensive capabilities of Southern armies. Foreign recognition and military assistance for the Confederacy seemed a distant hope. The Anaconda was strangling its prey.

With his elevation to general-in-chief of all Federal forces, Grant embarked on a coordinated strategy to put an end to the Confederacy. Major General William T. Sherman, Grant's most talented and trusted subordinate, would use Chattanooga as base of operations for a three-army drive at the heart of the Confederacy: "to get into the enemy's country as far as you can, inflicting all the damage you can against their war resources."

In the campaign that culminated in the capture of Atlanta and the epic march to Savannah and the sea, Sherman gained the enmity of generations of Southerners but took the art of war a step closer to the modern age. He cut loose from his bases of supply, confiscated the produce and livestock of the

"Grant habitually wears an expression as if he had determined to drive his head through a brick wall, and was about to do it."

LT. COL. THEODORE LYMAN
AIDE-DE-CAMP, GEN. GEORGE MEADE
ARMY OF THE POTOMAC

civilian population, and burned what could not be consumed. "Since they have been doing so much to destroy us and our government, we have to destroy them," Sherman told an aide. "In war everything is right."

Sherman's opponent in the Atlanta campaign was in many respects a Confederate McClellan. Like McClellan, General Joseph E. Johnston was a talented organizer and a figure of respect for the men in the ranks. Johnston was "almost worshiped by his troops," one veteran stated. "I do not believe there was a soldier in his army but would gladly have died for him." As McClellan had relinquished the initiative to Lee by his retreat in the Seven Days' Battles, so Johnston chose to wage a skillfully executed but strategically counterproductive withdrawal before Sherman's forces. Like McClellan, Johnston proved unable to maintain a good working relationship with his president and was ulti-

Renowned Civil War photographer Mathew Brady took this photograph of Gen. Ulysses S. Grant *(leaning against tree at left)* at his headquarters at Cold Harbor, Virginia, in June 1864. The portrait was taken eight days after the costly Union failure at Cold Harbor, about which General Grant later wrote, "I regret this assault more than any one I ever ordered."

mately relieved of command—a move that outraged the soldiers in the Army of Tennessee as much as McClellan's removal had angered the troops in the Army of the Potomac. Just as McClellan's successor, Ambrose Burnside, had damaged morale by his futile and bloody assault at Fredericksburg, so two years later Johnston's successor, General John Bell Hood, squandered his troops in the costly battles around Atlanta. Heavy losses, inadequate supplies, and low morale finally contributed to the decisive defeat of Hood's forces in the Franklin-Nashville campaign.

When Grant came east in the spring of 1864, the war in Virginia entered its last and deadliest phase. Resolved not to repeat the failures of earlier commanders, Grant pushed Lee's army back on Richmond. Forced to go on the defensive, Lee's troops fought from the cover of earthen and log breastworks, and inflicted terrible losses on the more numerous Federals, who were frequently compelled to entrench in turn. While many Federal officers despaired at the casualty rates in battles such as the Wilderness, Spotsylvania, and Cold Harbor, Grant knew that a war of attrition would inevitably work to the North's advantage. By late summer of 1864, Lee was confined to the defenses of Richmond and Petersburg, and the stage was set for the final campaign that ended in Confederate surrender at Appomattox.

Not long after the War, Lee remarked to his son Custis that during the last desperate march of the Army of Northern Virginia from Petersburg to Appomattox, "Every move I made was at once checkmated by Grant." That Grant was able to achieve what so many Federal leaders had tried and failed to do was not merely a function of his dogged determination, of a cohesive strategy, or of superior Federal numbers. Plain military necessity had at last weeded out most of the incompetents in the Union high command. By 1865 a new generation of Federal brigade and division commanders had come to the fore, many of them in their midtwenties. Major General Ranald Slidell Mackenzie, whom Grant regarded as "the most promising young officer in the army," had not even graduated from West Point until the summer of 1862. Young generals like James Wilson, Wesley Merritt, Emory Upton, and Nelson Miles had climbed the chain of command through ability, not political influence. They had arrived on the battlefield in time to help Grant put an end to the Confederacy.

EASTERN THEATER

Of the dozen bloodiest battles of the Civil War, nine were fought within the roughly 20,000-square-mile area that constituted the Eastern theater of operations. Seven of the nine engagements took place on Virginia soil. The locus of this carnage was as much the result of symbolic as of strategic considerations. In a defiant gesture during the War's second month, the new Confederacy transferred its capital from Montgomery, Alabama, to Richmond, Virginia—only 100 miles from the seat of the Federal government at Washington, D.C. The brash act set the stage for four bitter years of combat that ebbed and flowed across the ravaged farmland of the Old Dominion, and north into Maryland and Pennsylvania.

While the Federal government professed to fight for the preservation of the Republic and sought to restore the seceded states to the Union by force of arms, the South viewed the struggle as a battle for survival. "The Confederate Government is waging this war solely for self-defense," President Jefferson Davis claimed, "it has no designs of conquest or any other purpose than to secure peace."

To a large extent, the geography of the Eastern theater favored the defensive posture chosen by the Confederate leaders. The Blue Ridge and Allegheny mountain ranges, running southwest to northeast, narrowed the frontage the Confederates had to defend. And although the Union navy asserted control of the Atlantic coast and Chesapeake Bay early in the War, the bay's principal tributaries—the Potomac, Rappahannock, York, and James rivers—were natural east-west barriers that blocked the movement of invading Federal armies.

From the outset of the War, Union troops seized sections of Virginia's railroad system, which they augmented with the construction of numerous branch lines. The efficient U.S. Military Railroads service was capable of

transporting 800 tons of supplies a day to troops in the field. But despite the North's decided advantage in men and matériel, the Army of the Potomac—the principal Federal force in the Eastern theater—was unable to achieve a decisive victory on the battlefield in the first three years of fighting.

In the eight months that followed the Confederate victory at Bull Run on July 21, 1861, neither of the opposing commanders in the Eastern theater seemed disposed to risk another major engagement. George B. McClellan, commander of the Army of the Potomac, busied himself with organizational tasks. McClellan's opposite number, Confederate General Joseph E. Johnston, professed, "Our troops have always wished for the offensive." But it was General Johnston's withdrawal from Manassas—a scant 20 miles from Washington—that brought about active operations in the spring of 1862.

Rather than advance overland toward Johnston's new line on the Rappahannock, McClellan launched a massive amphibious expedition to the peninsula formed by the York and James rivers. The bold flanking maneuver forced the Confederates to rally to the defense of Richmond. But McClellan's ponderous advance up the peninsula stood in sharp contrast to the lightning maneuvers of Confederate commander Thomas J. "Stonewall" Jackson in the Shenandoah Valley. Jackson's victories in the Valley spurred the Union government's perennial fears for the safety of the city of Washington; 40,000 Federal troops earmarked for the advance on Richmond were held in reserve to protect the Northern capital.

In late June, the new commander of the Army of Northern Virginia, Robert E. Lee, launched a series of assaults that caused McClellan to abandon his position on the outskirts of Richmond. But Lee's success in the Seven Days' Battles was marred by lost opportunities that prevented the Confederates from smashing the Army of the Potomac. One Southern general complained, "the Confederate commanders knew no more about the topography of the country than they did about Central Africa."

Determined to improve his army's organization, Lee purged scores of incompetent, lackluster officers, replacing them with a hard-fighting cadre of dynamic, solid subordinates. In the Second Bull Run campaign of August 1862, Lee proved himself a master of the Napoleonic concept of *la manoeuvre sur les derrières*—the strategic envelopment of an opposing army's flank and rear. Using the Blue Ridge's easternmost range to screen his movements, Lee soundly thrashed the Yankees on the old battlefield of Bull Run.

Judging his foes "much weakened and demoralized," Lee crossed the Potomac into Maryland, carrying the war into Northern territory. On September 17, 1862, McClellan's Army of the Potomac squared off against Lee on the banks of Antietam Creek. The bloodiest day's fighting of the War was a tactical draw but caused Lee to abandon his invasion, a decision that denied the South hoped-for recognition from foreign powers and that paved the way for Abraham Lincoln's Emancipation Proclamation.

McClellan's reluctance to make decisive use of his superior numbers to pursue and engage the battered Army of Northern Virginia cost him his job. McClellan's successors in command of the Army of the Potomac, Ambrose Burnside and Joseph Hooker, followed Lincoln's mandate to assail Lee's forces. Both failed: Burnside in an unimaginative head-on assault at Fredericksburg on December 13, 1862, and Hooker in the cleverly conceived but poorly executed Chancellorsville campaign of May 1863. But while Lincoln's Eastern generals seemed incapable of vanquishing the Army of Northern Virginia, neither could Lee succeed in crippling Northern resolve to prosecute the War. In July 1863, a second invasion of the North was repulsed by Hooker's successor, General George Meade, at Gettysburg, Pennsylvania. It was the turning point of the war in the East.

In the spring of 1864, the principal Eastern armies seemed to be in a deadlock along the old line of the Rappahannock and its tributary, the Rapidan. But Lincoln had at last found a general determined to lead the Union to victory. Newly appointed as general-in-chief, Ulysses S. Grant launched a multifront offensive in the East and West, and personally took the field with Meade's Army of the Potomac. In a single month, Grant waged three pitched battles and half a dozen smaller engagements, relentlessly maneuvering around Lee's right flank, forcing the Army of Northern Virginia to withdraw to the fortifications of Richmond and Petersburg.

Confederate artillerist Edward Porter Alexander correctly recognized Grant's new strategy as "practically one of extermination—to reduce our numbers at all costs."

Grant indeed spent lives freely. In about 45 days of combat, he lost perhaps 68,000 men killed, wounded, and captured, while inflicting 42,000 casualties on the Confederates. As Grant well knew, his losses were replaceable, while Lee's were not. Although a bloody nine-month siege of Petersburg lay ahead, Northern victory appeared inevitable in the hard-fought Eastern theater.

"With the liberal supply of men and means which our superior resources ought to furnish, we will win in the long run," Meade wrote; "it is a question of tenacity and nerve, and it won't do to look behind, or to calculate the cost in blood and treasure." The resolution of Grant's grim war of attrition came at Appomattox on April 9, 1865, when the Army of Northern Virginia, the last hope of the Confederate cause, laid down its arms.

BATTLEFIELDS OF THE EASTERN THEATER

MARYLAND

CHESAPEAKE BAY

Potomac River

New Market

Luray

FISHER'S GAP

Aquia Creek

Aquia Landing

BLUE RIDGE MOUNTAINS

Culpeper Courthouse

Brandy Station

Rappahannock

Harrisonburg

Conrad's Store

CEDAR MOUNTAIN

Rapidan River

River

Fredericksburg

SWIFT RUN GAP

Cross Keys

Wilderness

Chancellorsville

Port Republic

Stanardsville

Spotsylvania Courthouse

BROWN'S GAP

Orange Courthouse

ROCKFISH GAP

Gordonsville

Pamunkey

Charlottesville

VIRGINIA & CENTRAL RR

River

ALEXANDRIA & ORANGE

RICHMOND, FREDERICKSBURG & POTOMAC RR

Hanover Junction

Hanover Courthouse

James River

Mechanicsville

Cold Harbor

White House

West Point

RICHMOND

Fair Oaks

Savage's Station

Seven Pines

York River

Glendale

Chickahominy River

Appomattox River

Drewry's Bluff

Malvern Hill

Appomattox Courthouse

Bermuda Hundred

Harrison's Landing

Williamsburg

Gloucester Point

Yorktown

RICHMOND & PETERSBURG RR

Bermuda Hundred

Burnt Chimneys

VIRGINIA & TENNESSEE RR

Sayler's Creek

Petersburg

Big Bethel

PETERSBURG & LYNCHBURG RR

Five Forks

NORFOLK & PETERSBURG RR

Hampton

FORT MONROE

Newport News

Hampton Roads

Nottoway

WELDON & PETERSBURG RR

Norfolk

RICHMOND & DANVILLE RR

Meherrin River

River

Suffolk

Dismal Swamp

Hicksford

SEABOARD

ROANOKE RR

Roanoke River

Ridgeway

Weldon

NORTH CAROLINA

Chowan River

ALBEMARLE SOUND

Scale in Miles

0   25   50   75

Through the spring of 1861, the Northern press and public angrily prodded President Abraham Lincoln and his government to launch the Union army into action. The presence of Confederate forces within a day's march of the nation's capital seemed intolerable, and pressure mounted for the Federals to attack, crush the Rebels, march on Richmond and end Secession with one blow. In early July the president, becoming impatient himself, ordered Brigadier General Irvin McDowell, his commander in the field, to go on the offensive.

McDowell was desperate. His army of about 35,000 men, forming around Washington, was by far the largest ever assembled in North America, but it was woefully ill-prepared for action—poorly trained, inadequately equipped, and led mostly by mossbacked old-timers and inexperienced amateurs. McDowell protested his unreadiness to Winfield Scott, the elderly and sage army chief. Scott pointed out that the enemy, too, lacked experience. "You are green, it is true," Scott observed, "but they are green also; you are all green alike."

Reluctantly, McDowell came up with a plan. He and his army would march westward from the Union camps around Washington, D.C., and clear the Confederates from their positions at Fairfax Courthouse and Centreville. From there, part of the Union force would move on the Confederate army thought to be camped behind a meandering stream called Bull Run, near the town of Manassas Junction. Another Federal column would attempt to outflank the Rebels, cut their main line of supply from Richmond, and force a withdrawal at least to the next natural line of defense, the Rappahannock River near Fredericksburg.

The main Confederate force, under Brigadier General Pierre Gustave Toutant Beauregard, was indeed near Manassas—a rail junction that afforded the Rebels excellent lines of communication. One track stretched south to Richmond, and another headed west into the Shenandoah Valley, connecting Beauregard's army with a smaller force commanded by General Joseph E. Johnston. In combination, the two Confederate armies totaled nearly as many men as the Federal army. When McDowell finally sent his brigades toward Bull Run on July 16, the stage was set for the first great battle of the War—a confused fight filled with miscalculations on both sides, and a surprisingly vicious one considering the inexperience of the two armies.

GEN. IRVIN McDOWELL, UNION COMMANDER AT BULL RUN

Briefly detraining during their dash to Bull Run, some of Johnston's troops from the Valley accept refreshments offered by local women at a stop on the Manassas Gap Railroad.

When McDowell's Federals started westward toward Fairfax Courthouse and Centreville on July 16 and 17, Confederate President Jefferson Davis and his chief military adviser, Robert E. Lee, were still desperately speeding reinforcements from all over the South through Richmond to Manassas. At the same time, other small units, including Theophilus Holmes' brigade from Aquia Creek and the Hampton Legion from Richmond, also headed for the contested ground. Then, as the Union attack loomed, Johnston in the Shenandoah Valley swiftly put his four brigades aboard trains for the 50-mile trip to join Beauregard's army.

26

OPENING MOVEMENTS, JULY 21

Probing Federal attacks on Mitchell's and Blackburn's fords on July 18 ran into fierce opposition, and McDowell gave up any idea of a direct movement toward Manassas Junction. Instead, he decided on a wide flanking movement around the Confederate left. On the morning of July 21, the leading Union brigades of Colonels Ambrose Burnside and Andrew Porter (*blue*) splashed across Bull Run at Sudley Ford, well to the north of Beauregard's defensive positions. Heintzelman's division followed and reinforced Burnside and

Porter while other Federal units moved down the Warrenton Turnpike to threaten the Stone Bridge, and still others feinted toward the main fords farther downstream. The Confederate brigades (*red*) were caught badly out of position, spread over a six-mile front with most troops on the right, where Beauregard was convinced the main Federal blow must fall. Only Nathan Evans' small two-regiment brigade moved at first to meet the dangerous Union thrust that threatened to turn the lightly held Rebel left.

ORDER OF BATTLE

CONFEDERATE FORCES
JOHNSTON

ARMY OF THE POTOMAC
BEAUREGARD
21,800 MEN

FIRST BRIGADE	SECOND BRIGADE	THIRD BRIGADE	FOURTH BRIGADE
BONHAM	EWELL	D. R. JONES	LONGSTREET

FIFTH BRIGADE	SIXTH BRIGADE	"SEVENTH BRIGADE"	"RESERVE BRIGADE"
COCKE	EARLY	EVANS	HOLMES

ARMY OF THE SHENANDOAH
JOHNSTON
9,500 MEN

FIRST BRIGADE	SECOND BRIGADE	THIRD BRIGADE	FOURTH BRIGADE
JACKSON	BARTOW	BEE	KIRBY SMITH

ADDITIONAL FORCES

Several unbrigaded infantry, cavalry, and artillery units
including the Hampton Legion and Stuart's and Radford's Virginia cavalry regiments.

UNION ARMY
McDOWELL
35,700 MEN

FIRST DIVISION: TYLER	SECOND DIVISION: HUNTER	THIRD DIVISION: HEINTZELMAN
Brigades: KEYES, SCHENCK, SHERMAN, RICHARDSON	*Brigades:* PORTER, BURNSIDE	*Brigades:* FRANKLIN, WILLCOX, HOWARD

FOURTH DIVISION: RUNYON	FIFTH DIVISION: MILES
EIGHT UNBRIGADED REGIMENTS	*Brigades:* BLENKER, DAVIES

Beauregard doffs his cap to a regiment of boisterous Mississippi soldiers as they pass in ragged review, brandishing bowie knives. The Louisiana general's informal style of leadership kept the spirits of his men high; he often dropped in on their camps to mix with the rank and file.

The three fast-acting, resolute Confederate officers who wheeled their brigades to meet the main Federal attack are shown at right. Evans, a West Point graduate, was a gruff, heavy-drinking South Carolinian, known as Shanks for his skinny bowlegs. Bee, also a West Pointer, was known for his courage and independence. Bartow, who had energetically taught himself soldiering, was a lawyer in Savannah before the War. Both Bee and Bartow were mortally wounded at Bull Run.

COL. NATHAN G. EVANS

BRIG. GEN. BARNARD E. BEE

MATTHEWS HILL

Only minutes after Burnside's and Porter's brigades had crossed Sudley Ford and turned southward across rolling, partially wooded ground, Evans threw his brigade in their path on Matthews Hill. There Evans' small force, vastly outnumbered, held the Federals at bay until he was reinforced on his right, first by Bee's brigade, then by Bartow's. Together the three Confederate brigades fought furiously to hold off three times as many attacking Union troops and stalled McDowell's flanking movement for almost two hours. Finally, however, Federal pressure was too great. Porter's and Burnside's brigades threatened the left flank of the Confederate line, and Union brigades led by Colonels William Tecumseh Sherman and Erasmus D. Keyes that had crossed Bull Run just above the Stone Bridge were moving on the Confederates' rear. By 11:00 a.m., Evans, Bee, and Bartow were forced to withdraw their remaining troops back across Warrenton Turnpike and up the lower slope of Henry House Hill. But by then, Beauregard had realized the extent of the threat to his left flank and had begun to send more reinforcements in that direction. First to arrive was the so-called Hampton Legion, organized and led by the wealthy planter Colonel Wade Hampton. His small, 600-man unit was soon followed by the large brigade commanded by Thomas J. Jackson, who led his men smartly through the hot morning toward the slopes of Henry House Hill.

COL. FRANCIS S. BARTOW

In the opening phase of the battle, the regiments of Burnside's brigade—foreground in the painting below—advance past the Matthews farmhouse (also shown in the photo at right) toward the Confederate line *(background)*.

Disaster strikes the Federal batteries commanded by Ricketts and Griffin as the 33d Virginia charges their flank. Because the Virginians wore blue uniforms, the artillerymen held their fire and lost their guns as a result.

HENRY HOUSE HILL

By late morning, the Federals had clearly gained the upper hand. The leading brigades had shoved aside the badly mauled troops of Bee, Bartow, and Evans, and heavy Union reinforcements led by Sherman, Franklin, and others had advanced across the turnpike and were heading up Henry House Hill. With the Federal infantry came powerful artillery support—20 or more guns commanded by a pair of daring and able officers, Captains Charles Griffin and James B. Ricketts, who deployed their cannon near the crest of the hill and began pounding the Confederate line. But around 2:30 p.m., the momentum shifted. Disobeying the orders of Jackson—who had just earned his nickname by standing "like a stone wall"—Colonel Arthur Cummings boldly led his 33d Virginia against the Union batteries. This headlong attack by the Virginians overwhelmed the exposed artillery and routed a battalion of U.S. Marines and the 11th New York, which were supporting the Union guns.

General Joseph E. Johnston *(foreground)*, arriving at the threatened Confederate left flank, helps reorganize the sagging defense by rallying a Georgia regiment while Colonel Bartow, waving a flag *(left)*, gallops through enemy fire to regroup his hard-hit brigade.

Trying to recapture the Union artillery, Vermont and Maine regiments of Colonel Oliver O. Howard's brigade charge up Henry House Hill. The New Englanders were soon flanked and routed by Edmund Kirby Smith's brigade, which rushed to reinforce Jackson.

Fleeing in panic from Bull Run in what became known as "the great skedaddle," Union troops and supply wagons race eastward along one of the roads leading to Centreville and Washington.

Trying to prevent a total rout, a sword-waving Colonel Louis Blenker orders his New York troops, stationed near Centreville, to fire on the Confederate cavalry that spearheaded the pursuit of the Federal forces.

FEDERAL RETREAT

Having shifted large reserves to Jackson's left, Beauregard sent fresh troops moving down Henry House Hill and the adjacent Bald Hill and Chinn Ridge. Kirby Smith's brigade, followed by Colonel Jubal A. Early's, slammed into Howard's weary men and routed them. Soon more Federal units, disorganized and disheartened, began to leave the field. Now Beauregard ordered a general attack that caved in the entire right wing of McDowell's army. The Federal soldiers threw away their guns and packs and fled, some by way of Sudley

Ford, others by the shorter route across the Stone Bridge. "The retreat soon became a rout," McDowell later said, "and this soon degenerated still further into a panic." Beauregard ordered a pursuit; but his troops, too, were tired, and the Union army—less 3,000 killed, wounded, or captured—managed to straggle back into Washington over the next several days. The Confederates lost fewer men, however—perhaps 2,000—and gained a glorious victory that put an end to Northern expectations of a short war.

Major General John Pope
was named commander of
the Union's new Army of
Virginia after leading Federal troops to victory at
New Madrid and Corinth
along the Mississippi River
in the Western theater.

UNION	CONFEDERATE	
→	→	JUNE 26–AUG. 9
◄----	◄----	AUG. 10–27
•••••►	◄••••	AUG. 28 & 29

0   5   10   15   20

Scale in Miles

In the first stage of his advance
from Richmond, Lee rushed
Jackson's command to Gordonsville via the Virginia Central Railroad in mid-July. A. P. Hill followed and joined Jackson in
repulsing the Federals at Cedar
Mountain on August 9. Then Lee
sent Jackson circling around
Pope's army and into its rear via
Thoroughfare Gap. After raiding
the Union supply depot at Manassas Junction, Jackson took up
positions northwest of Bull Run.
Lee and Longstreet, following
the same route, caught up on August 29, uniting the army's two
wings. In mid-August, meanwhile,
Pope had ordered the scattered
corps of McDowell, Sigel, and
Banks to concentrate north of
the Rappahannock River. Pope
also received reinforcements
shipped up the Potomac—most
notably Heintzelman's III Corps
and Porter's V Corps from McClellan's army, which was now with-
drawing from the Peninsula. But
not until August 26, after Jackson's raid, did Pope come up with
a plan. Believing he could destroy Jackson, he ordered his dis-
persed forces to find and attack
the waiting Confederates.

Samuel Crawford's Federals charge through woods and over a rail fence at Cedar Mountain, routing Jackson's left flank, including the famed Stonewall Brigade, which up to that time had never been driven from the field.

In a sketch done for a Northern magazine, Federal ambulances line up near a farmhouse used as a hospital at Cedar Mountain. The numbers keyed the scene for the magazine's editors; for example, the *4* indicates Union guns firing at Confederate positions north of Cedar Run.

The first battle of the campaign flared at Cedar Mountain on the afternoon of August 9 when Jackson and A. P. Hill, probing northward from Gordonsville, ran into Nathaniel Banks' corps, which was leading Pope's slow, strung-out advance. The Federals, despite knowing they were outnumbered more than two to one, launched an attack—which nearly succeeded. Lying undetected in thick woods, Crawford's 1,700-man brigade suddenly burst upon the Confederate left, routing the brigades of Ronald, Garnett, and Taliaferro of Winder's division. But the Federals lacked the reserves to exploit Crawford's breakthrough. As the Union attack faltered, Jackson counterattacked with the brigades of Branch, Archer, and Pender of Hill's division, smashing Crawford's brigade and driving Banks' forces from the field. It was a badly mismanaged battle on both sides that left 3,700 dead and wounded.

General Charles Winder, one of Jackson's most trusted subordinates, was killed by a shell at Cedar Mountain shortly before the attack that shattered his division.

ORDER OF BATTLE

ARMY OF NORTHERN VIRGINIA
LEE
55,000 MEN

LEFT WING (FIRST CORPS)
JACKSON

W. B. TALIAFERRO'S DIVISION

BAYLOR'S BRIGADE
JOHNSON'S BRIGADE
A. G. TALIAFERRO'S
BRIGADE
STARKE'S BRIGADE

A. P. HILL'S DIVISION

BRANCH'S BRIGADE
ARCHER'S BRIGADE
PENDER'S BRIGADE
FIELD'S BRIGADE
GREGG'S BRIGADE
THOMAS' BRIGADE

EWELL'S DIVISION

LAWTON'S BRIGADE
EARLY'S BRIGADE
TRIMBLE'S BRIGADE
STRONG'S BRIGADE

RIGHT WING (SECOND CORPS)
LONGSTREET

R. H. ANDERSON'S DIVISION

ARMISTEAD'S BRIGADE
MAHONE'S BRIGADE
WRIGHT'S BRIGADE

D. R. JONES' DIVISION

BENNING'S BRIGADE
DRAYTON'S BRIGADE
G. T. ANDERSON'S BRIGADE

WILCOX'S DIVISION

WILCOX'S BRIGADE
PRYOR'S BRIGADE
FEATHERSTON'S BRIGADE

HOOD'S/EVANS' DIVISION

HOOD'S BRIGADE
LAW'S BRIGADE
STEVENS' BRIGADE

KEMPER'S DIVISION

CORSE'S BRIGADE
JENKINS' BRIGADE
HUNTON'S BRIGADE

CAVALRY
STUART

HAMPTON'S BRIGADE   F. LEE'S BRIGADE

ROBERTSON'S BRIGADE

ARMY OF VIRGINIA
POPE
70,000 MEN

I CORPS SIGEL

FIRST DIVISION: SCHENCK
Brigades: STAHEL, McLEAN

SECOND DIVISION: VON STEINWEHR
(KOLTES' BRIGADE ONLY)

THIRD DIVISION: SCHURZ
Brigades: SCHIMMELFENNIG, KRZYZANOWSKI, MILROY

CAVALRY BRIGADE: BEARDSLEY

II CORPS BANKS

FIRST DIVISION: WILLIAMS
Brigades: CRAWFORD, GORDON

SECOND DIVISION: GREENE
Brigades: CANDY, SCHLAUDECKER, TAIT

CAVALRY BRIGADE: BUFORD

III CORPS McDOWELL

FIRST DIVISION: KING
Brigades: HATCH, DOUBLEDAY, PATRICK, GIBBON

SECOND DIVISION: RICKETTS
Brigades: DURYEA, TOWER, STILES, THOBURN

REYNOLDS' DIVISION
Brigades: MEADE, SEYMOUR, JACKSON

CAVALRY BRIGADE: BAYARD

RESERVE CORPS STURGIS
(PIATT'S BRIGADE ONLY)

from: ARMY OF THE POTOMAC

III CORPS HEINTZELMAN

FIRST DIVISION: KEARNY
Brigades: ROBINSON, BIRNEY, POE

SECOND DIVISION: HOOKER
Brigades: GROVER, TAYLOR, CARR

V CORPS PORTER

FIRST DIVISION: MORELL
Brigades: ROBERTS, GRIFFIN, BUTTERFIELD

SECOND DIVISION: SYKES
Brigades: BUCHANAN, CHAPMAN, WARREN

VI CORPS
(TAYLOR'S BRIGADE ONLY)

IX CORPS (UNDER RENO'S COMMAND)

FIRST DIVISION: STEVENS
Brigades: CHRIST, LEASURE, FARNSWORTH

SECOND DIVISION: RENO
Brigades: NAGLE, FERRERO

Battle flag flying, jubilant Georgia infantrymen of Colonel Evander Law's brigade fire down on Ricketts' Federals, who had arrived to block Thoroughfare Gap in the Bull Run Mountains on August 28, two days after Jackson had gotten through. Law's Georgians reopened the gap, allowing Longstreet's command to pass through and join Jackson.

BRAWNER'S FARM, AUGUST 28

After falling back from Manassas Junction in three columns on August 27, Jackson reunited his force along Stony Ridge just north of the Warrenton Turnpike near Groveton. There he waited behind an unfinished railroad embankment for Lee and Longstreet. But, before their arrival, the combative Jackson touched off the battle on the afternoon of August 28 when the four Federal brigades of King's division, marching east along the turnpike to join Pope in Centreville, passed Jackson's hidden positions. Concerned that time was now on the side of Pope, Jackson decided to strike. He let the first Union brigade of John Hatch go by, then ordered his batteries to shell John Gibbon's brigade, which followed after. Gibbon sent a line of skirmishers advancing toward the guns up a slope on a farm owned by John Brawner—and found himself facing six Confederate brigades from Taliaferro's and Ewell's divisions. While the two forces traded volleys from lines only 75 yards apart, Abner Doubleday, whose Federal brigade had been following Gibbon's, rushed up to help. The battle sputtered out only when darkness came and the men found themselves aiming at each other's muzzle flashes. The Federals finally fell back, and the exhausted Confederates did not pursue. Casualties were heavy—about 1,300 on each side—with Gibbon losing more than 900 of his 2,100 men. Jackson also lost two division commanders, Generals Ewell and Taliaferro, both of whom were wounded.

FEDERAL ATTACKS, AUGUST 29

After Jackson revealed his position at Brawner's Farm, Pope ordered all available units to converge on the Bull Run battlefield. He failed, however, to outline a coherent plan of attack. The result was a series of piecemeal assaults that never employed more than a fraction of the Union strength. Most of the attacks were thrown back by murderous fire from Confederate infantry entrenched behind the ready-made bulwark of the railroad embankment. On the Federal right, Grover's brigade of Hooker's division cut through Lawton's first and second lines but, unsupported, was stopped by the third line. On the Federals' far right, Philip Kearny led a furious rush that nearly overwhelmed Gregg's South Carolinians, but the Federals were thrown back by A. P. Hill's reserves. Meanwhile, unknown to Pope, Longstreet's entire wing had arrived on the Confederate right, ready to outflank and roll up the Federal left. A late-afternoon probe by troops from Hood's division was met head-on in a brutal encounter with Hatch's division (formerly King's) that ended in a stalemate after sundown. South of the turnpike, Fitz-John Porter's V Corps remained inactive. Having belatedly received attack orders that arrived almost at dusk, Porter refused to advance, in part because of ominous signs that a huge force was massing on the Confederate right.

Confederate infantry, from the cover of the railroad embankment, hurl rocks into a wave of Federal attackers. The Confederates also had the advantage of the high ground provided by the ridge line that Jackson had chosen for his defensive position.

Philip Kearny, who led the attack on the Rebel left on August 29, was killed three days later in a brief, bloody fight that followed the main battle. Even the Confederates mourned the death of so gallant a man.

A photograph made after the battle shows the Warrenton Turnpike running past a farm *(foreground)* and the railroad cut atop the distant slope.

64

LONGSTREET'S ATTACK, AUGUST 30

Pope, still unaware of Longstreet's presence, massed virtually his entire army north of the
Warrenton Turnpike on the
morning of the 30th for what, he
thought, would be a final, crushing attack on Jackson's line. The
leading Federal units were engaged in storming the railroad
cut when Longstreet, shortly
before 4:00 p.m., launched his
massive and unexpected attack.
Anderson's division and part of
Hood's surged forward north of
the turnpike, crossing in front
of Jackson's embattled right. More
of Hood's men smashed through
Warren's New York brigade—virtually the only Federals still
south of the pike. Farther south,
Longstreet's divisions, led by
Jones and Kemper, advanced unopposed toward Chinn Ridge in
a dangerous flanking movement.
By 5:00, Pope, at last realizing
what was afoot, dispatched reinforcements, first from Sigel's and
McDowell's corps, across the pike
to Chinn Ridge and Henry House
Hill to slow the Confederate attack. These and other troops put
up a fighting withdrawal that
slowed Longstreet's advance long
enough to save the Federal army
from annihilation.

In one of the last attacks
by the Federals during
the afternoon of August
30, Lieutenant Colonel
William Chapman *(on
borseback, right)* leads
his Regular Army brigade
in a charge on Jackson's
line. "The slope was
swept by a hurricane of
death," a Union survivor
said, "and each minute
seemed 20 hours long."

66

A panoramic view of the battle sketched from the slope of Henry House Hill in midafternoon, August 30, shows Pope's line on the ridge in the middle distance facing Jackson's troops, in their positions on the wooded slope beyond. At right is the Stone House; at left, Milroy's brigade moves toward Chinn Ridge.

Federal infantrymen flee in panic from onrushing Confederates despite the efforts of a mounted officer to stem the rout.

CONFEDERATE ATTACKS AND FEDERAL RETREAT

Shortly after 5:00 p.m., the bulk of Longstreet's command hurled itself against the hastily formed Federal line on Chinn Ridge. In less than an hour, despite a ferocious defense, the Confederates had control of the ridge. Now Pope's entire left began to give way, the troops retreating toward the turnpike. About 6:00, Jackson's troops attacked the center and right of Pope's army. Some Federal units, including Gibbon's brigade and Kearny's men, held for a time, but eventually they were driven back toward Bull Run and the Stone Bridge. Saving the Federals from complete disaster were brigades from the divisions of Reynolds, Sykes, Reno, and Schurz, who stubbornly held the Manassas-Sudley Road, then the slopes of Henry House Hill, preventing the Confederate right from reaching the turnpike and clamping shut the Federal line of withdrawal. As dusk fell, the Confederate attack ended, and Pope's army made an orderly retreat. By midnight, all but a few stragglers were across Bull Run and trudging toward Centreville and Washington. The casualties in the two-day battle were horrendous. Pope's ill-led army lost 14,462 men, Lee's forces 9,474.

ANTIETAM CAMPAIGN

Immediately after his stunning victory at Bull Run, Robert E. Lee decided to keep the initiative by thrusting into Maryland. Although his army was depleted and exhausted, its morale was soaring, and the plan offered several attractions. Northern Virginia had been stripped of foodstuffs; Maryland held the promise of a rich autumn harvest to feed the Confederate troops. Lee's move north would draw Federal forces away from war-ravaged Confederate territory and forestall any advance on Richmond. And, possibly, his invasion of the Union would so galvanize discontent over the War in the North that Lincoln would be forced to sue for peace.

Soon after Lee crossed the Potomac River into Maryland on September 4, the Union army, reorganized once again under George McClellan, moved westward to intercept the Confederates. Within two weeks, the rival forces would collide along Antietam Creek near the dusty village of Sharpsburg. The battle there would rank as the bloodiest one-day encounter of the entire Civil War.

A Federal scout shoots at men of Lee's army as they wade across the Potomac at White's Ford on the night of September 4, 1862.

After a final clash with John Pope's rear guard at Chantilly on September 1, Lee marched his army northward, crossing the Potomac at two fords near Leesburg and moving on to Frederick, in Maryland. There, on September 10, he daringly ordered a temporary four-way split of his army. James Longstreet and D. H. Hill headed north to threaten Hagerstown and southern Pennsylvania. Stonewall Jackson, John Walker, and Lafayette McLaws took three widely divergent routes to surprise the Federal garrison at Harpers Ferry, capture that Union outpost, and open a Confederate supply line through the Shenandoah Valley. On September 5, McClellan had taken up the pursuit, dividing his divisions into three wings that advanced toward Frederick on a front 25 miles wide. Ambrose Burnside and his column hooked northward to protect the Baltimore & Ohio tracks. Edwin Sumner marched his wing on two middle routes via Gaithersburg and Darnestown. William Franklin's wing hugged the Maryland shore of the Potomac. The advance guard approached Frederick on September 11, the day after Lee's divisions had left the city. There McClellan learned of the Confederate plans from a copy of Lee's orders that somehow had been lost, and he pushed his army westward hoping to catch the Rebels while they were still spread across the countryside. But Lee, suspecting the Federal intentions, ordered McLaws and Jackson to speed up the capture of Harpers Ferry, and Longstreet and D. H. Hill to block the Federal advance at South Mountain to gain time. After an opening clash there on September 14, Lee's army fell back toward Sharpsburg to await the oncoming Federals.

Troops of Jacob Cox's division storm a hill defended by Samuel Garland's Confederates during the Federal assault at Fox's Gap. In the left foreground, two soldiers attend their wounded regimental commander, Rutherford B. Hayes.

In a Federal assault at dusk on the north side of Turner's Gap, Pennsylvanians of John Hatch's division overrun Alabama troops who had been firing from behind stone outcroppings on the gap's wooded crest.

The first crisis of Lee's campaign came when McClellan arrived on September 14 with three Federal corps at South Mountain, a long ridge that stretched roughly 40 miles from the Potomac River to Pennsylvania. With Jackson absent at Harpers Ferry and other units still scattered, Lee ordered the few troops available to hold the South Mountain passes at all costs until he could reunite his army. The initial Federal attack came shortly after dawn, when Cox's division from Reno's IX Corps tried to outflank the Confederates holding Turner's Gap by taking nearby Fox's Gap. After a sharp two-hour battle, the Federals drove off Garland's brigade, and by midday the lead elements of Reno's corps had passed through the gap and were advancing north along a ridge toward Turner's Gap. The Federals were stopped, however, by D. H. Hill's division and just-arriving troops from Longstreet's command. This attack stymied, McClellan ordered Gibbon's brigade to march straight for Turner's Gap while the rest of Hooker's I Corps hit the Confederates from the north. Gibbon could make little progress, but eventually attacks by Hatch and Meade forced the Confederates from the pass—only to have darkness stop the fighting and allow the troops of Hill and Longstreet to withdraw in good order. The main Union success came at Crampton's Gap six miles to the south, where Franklin's VI Corps easily defeated a handful of Confederate defenders. But Franklin failed to follow up, losing a chance to hit McLaws' lone division marching up from Harpers Ferry.

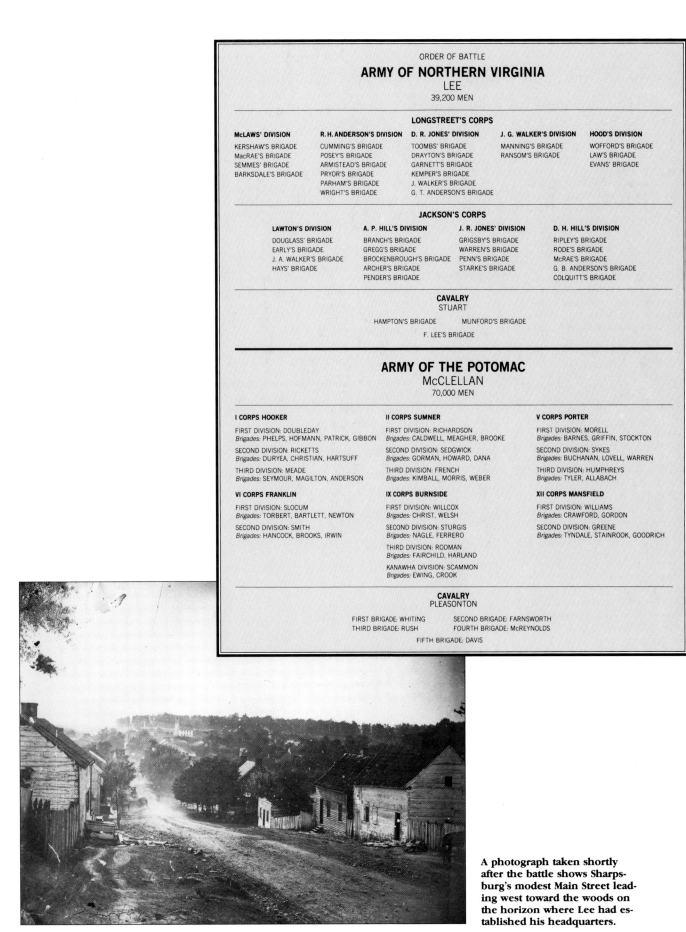

ORDER OF BATTLE

ARMY OF NORTHERN VIRGINIA
LEE
39,200 MEN

LONGSTREET'S CORPS

McLAWS' DIVISION	R. H. ANDERSON'S DIVISION	D. R. JONES' DIVISION	J. G. WALKER'S DIVISION	HOOD'S DIVISION
KERSHAW'S BRIGADE	CUMMING'S BRIGADE	TOOMBS' BRIGADE	MANNING'S BRIGADE	WOFFORD'S BRIGADE
MacRAE'S BRIGADE	POSEY'S BRIGADE	DRAYTON'S BRIGADE	RANSOM'S BRIGADE	LAW'S BRIGADE
SEMMES' BRIGADE	ARMISTEAD'S BRIGADE	GARNETT'S BRIGADE		EVANS' BRIGADE
BARKSDALE'S BRIGADE	PRYOR'S BRIGADE	KEMPER'S BRIGADE		
	PARHAM'S BRIGADE	J. WALKER'S BRIGADE		
	WRIGHT'S BRIGADE	G. T. ANDERSON'S BRIGADE		

JACKSON'S CORPS

LAWTON'S DIVISION	A. P. HILL'S DIVISION	J. R. JONES' DIVISION	D. H. HILL'S DIVISION
DOUGLASS' BRIGADE	BRANCH'S BRIGADE	GRIGSBY'S BRIGADE	RIPLEY'S BRIGADE
EARLY'S BRIGADE	GREGG'S BRIGADE	WARREN'S BRIGADE	RODE'S BRIGADE
J. A. WALKER'S BRIGADE	BROCKENBROUGH'S BRIGADE	PENN'S BRIGADE	McRAE'S BRIGADE
HAYS' BRIGADE	ARCHER'S BRIGADE	STARKE'S BRIGADE	G. B. ANDERSON'S BRIGADE
	PENDER'S BRIGADE		COLQUITT'S BRIGADE

CAVALRY
STUART

HAMPTON'S BRIGADE   MUNFORD'S BRIGADE

F. LEE'S BRIGADE

ARMY OF THE POTOMAC
McCLELLAN
70,000 MEN

I CORPS HOOKER

FIRST DIVISION: DOUBLEDAY
Brigades: PHELPS, HOFMANN, PATRICK, GIBBON

SECOND DIVISION: RICKETTS
Brigades: DURYEA, CHRISTIAN, HARTSUFF

THIRD DIVISION: MEADE
Brigades: SEYMOUR, MAGILTON, ANDERSON

VI CORPS FRANKLIN

FIRST DIVISION: SLOCUM
Brigades: TORBERT, BARTLETT, NEWTON

SECOND DIVISION: SMITH
Brigades: HANCOCK, BROOKS, IRWIN

II CORPS SUMNER

FIRST DIVISION: RICHARDSON
Brigades: CALDWELL, MEAGHER, BROOKE

SECOND DIVISION: SEDGWICK
Brigades: GORMAN, HOWARD, DANA

THIRD DIVISION: FRENCH
Brigades: KIMBALL, MORRIS, WEBER

IX CORPS BURNSIDE

FIRST DIVISION: WILLCOX
Brigades: CHRIST, WELSH

SECOND DIVISION: STURGIS
Brigades: NAGLE, FERRERO

THIRD DIVISION: RODMAN
Brigades: FAIRCHILD, HARLAND

KANAWHA DIVISION: SCAMMON
Brigades: EWING, CROOK

V CORPS PORTER

FIRST DIVISION: MORELL
Brigades: BARNES, GRIFFIN, STOCKTON

SECOND DIVISION: SYKES
Brigades: BUCHANAN, LOVELL, WARREN

THIRD DIVISION: HUMPHREYS
Brigades: TYLER, ALLABACH

XII CORPS MANSFIELD

FIRST DIVISION: WILLIAMS
Brigades: CRAWFORD, GORDON

SECOND DIVISION: GREENE
Brigades: TYNDALE, STAINROOK, GOODRICH

CAVALRY
PLEASONTON

FIRST BRIGADE: WHITING   SECOND BRIGADE: FARNSWORTH
THIRD BRIGADE: RUSH   FOURTH BRIGADE: McREYNOLDS

FIFTH BRIGADE: DAVIS

A photograph taken shortly after the battle shows Sharpsburg's modest Main Street leading west toward the woods on the horizon where Lee had established his headquarters.

73

OPENING SITUATION, SEPTEMBER 17

Lee was tempted to retreat into Virginia after the Federals broke through at South Mountain, but he became his usual combative self after receiving news that Jackson had triumphed at Harpers Ferry. Now determined to fight, Lee issued orders for all units to concentrate at the town of Sharpsburg. By first light on September 17, most of his army was ranged on a ridge north and east of the town, with Jackson on the left flank and Longstreet in the center. The right was left lightly defended in anticipation of the late arrival of A. P.

Hill's division from Harpers Ferry. Predictably, McClellan moved slowly, giving Lee time to concentrate and deploy. Not until the afternoon of September 16, 24 hours after reaching Antietam Creek, did McClellan begin issuing orders for an attack the next day. He moved two of his corps, commanded by Hooker and Mansfield, across Antietam Creek to the north to attack the Confederate left. Two other corps would hold the center to wait for developments while Burnside staged a diversion by advancing across the creek on Lee's right.

Brigadier General John Gibbon's troops earned the nickname Iron Brigade for their performance at Turner's Gap. On the morning of September 17, the reputation of his command was tested again in the bitter fighting along the Hagerstown Turnpike.

FEDERAL I CORPS ATTACK

Hooker's I Corps launched the Federal attack at 5:30 a.m. with Doubleday's division pushing south on the Federal far right, Ricketts' division advancing through the East Woods, and Meade's division attacking in the center. Savage fighting soon developed on Ricketts' front in the soon-to-be-infamous Cornfield. A Federal cannonade blasted the Confederates hidden in the head-high stalks, and the Union brigades rushed through—only to be met by deadly volleys from Alexander Lawton's Confederates. A ferocious seesaw fight continued around the East Woods and along the eastern edge of the Cornfield until 7:00 a.m., when the bloodletting finally forced a stalemate. A few hundred yards to the west, on the Federal right, Doubleday's division, with Gibbon's brigade in the lead, thrust a mile down both sides of the Hagerstown Turnpike but then was raked by Confederate fire from the brigades of David R. Jones' division positioned west of the turnpike. Supported by heavy artillery fire, Gibbon's men pushed the Rebels back. On all fronts, Jackson's Confederates teetered near collapse. Then Hood's division, which had been held in reserve, charged the Federals' right and center, while D. H. Hill's division attacked the Federal left. Hood's men sent the Yankees reeling until they were stopped by Meade's division at the Cornfield's northern edge.

Spearheading the opening assault, troops from the Federal I Corps charge through the bullet-swept Cornfield.

BRIG. GEN. WILLIAM E. STARKE

Dead Confederates of Starke's Louisiana Brigade lie in rows along the rail fence by the Hagerstown Turnpike, killed by the advancing troops of Abner Doubleday's division. General William Starke *(above, right)*, a rising star in the Army of Northern Virginia, was fatally wounded in the fight.

Legend:
- WOODS
- ORCHARD
- CORNFIELD
- GRASS
- STUBBLE
- PLOWED

I CORPS HOOKER

XII CORPS MANSFIELD

WILLIAMS

GORDON

CRAWFORD

MEADE

GOODRICH

GREENE

TYNDALE

STAINROOK

SMOKETOWN ROAD

S. Poffenberger Farm

GIBBON

HAGERSTOWN TURNPIKE

West Woods

HOOD

East Woods

II CORPS SEDGWICK

GRIGSBY   EARLY

RIPLEY

Mumma Farm

Dunker Church

COLQUITT

MCRAE

Roulette Farm

S.D. LEE

D.H. HILL

0   1   2

Scale in Miles

FEDERAL XII CORPS ATTACK

Idle during Hooker's attack, Joseph Mansfield's XII Corps advanced around 7:30 a.m. After a confusing start, the two Federal divisions picked up momentum, first pushing Hood's exhausted troops from the East Woods and the Cornfield and then engaging D. H. Hill's brigades in a bloody standoff. Then a regiment in William McRae's Confederate brigade, about to be flanked, broke and ran, carrying most of the brigade with it. Through the gap poured 1,700 Federals of Tyndale's and Stainrook's brigades led by General George Greene. Soon Hood's and D. H. Hill's men were streaming back to the West Woods. But after reaching the high ground around the Dunker Church, Greene's Federals, now taking fire from the woods and low on ammunition, faltered—as did the entire XII Corps assault. Around 9:00 a.m., the fighting subsided, and a lull settled over the battlefield.

Troops from one of Greene's Federal brigades pause near the blazing ruins of the Mumma farmhouse and its outbuildings, torched by the retreating Confederates to prevent Federal sharpshooters from using them as cover.

Burning of Mr. Mumma's houses and barns at the fight of the 17th Sept.

Deploying in dense ranks near a corner of the East Woods *(left)*, troops from the Federal XII Corps exchange fire with Confederates defending the northern edge of the Cornfield. The XII Corps commander, General Joseph Mansfield *(right)*, a Regular Army engineer, had taken command only two days earlier. Shortly after sending his men into battle, he was mortally wounded in the chest.

MAJ. GEN. JOSEPH MANSFIELD

Men of Greene's Federal division charge past the tiny, shell-shot Dunker Church after helping to drive Stonewall Jackson's troops from the hotly contested open fields to the northeast. The caisson at far left, abandoned by retreating gunners of Stephen D. Lee's Confederate batteries, marked the farthest Federal advance during the early-morning attacks on the Confederate left. After gaining the plateau near the church, Greene's troops were stopped by Rebel fire. But they managed to hold their position and later aided the attack by General William French's division *(next pages).*

In earthworks above the stone wall on Marye's Heights, men of Robert Ransom's 24th North Carolina pour fire into dense lines of Federal troops struggling up the slope. The battlefield artist, an English journalist, made note of the shallow ravine in which some Union troops took cover.

Beneath a hill held by Jackson's artillery, Federal burial parties lay the dead to rest the day after the battle. Many of the corpses had been stripped of uniforms and shoes during the night by Confederate scavengers.

CHANCELLORSVILLE

The dreadful butchery at Fredericksburg ignited such an outcry in the North that Lincoln was again forced to change commanders. Out was Ambrose Burnside, in was one of his subordinates—and severest critics—Joseph Hooker. It was a controversial appointment. Hooker was thought to drink heavily and was known to be both arrogant and ambitious. But he had also shown signs of being an aggressive general who deserved his nickname, Fighting Joe.

Hooker energetically revitalized Burnside's tired and dispirited army. As the Union force spent the winter in quarters around Falmouth north of Fredericksburg, the new commander vastly improved sanitation, diet, and morale. By the early spring of 1863, he could boast that he had "the finest army on the planet," and added that he would soon lead it to Richmond and beyond.

Robert E. Lee's Army of Northern Virginia was, as usual, ill fed, ill shod, ill clothed, and generally miserable in its winter camps across the Rappahannock around Fredericksburg. It was also smaller than before; Lee had sent Longstreet south with two divisions to forage for provisions and keep an eye on the Federals along the Virginia-North Carolina coast. But even this reduced force could easily hold the vastly improved earthworks the men had been digging in and around Fredericksburg ever since the December battle. For the Federals, another frontal attack was out of the question. Hooker's only option was to outflank Lee, by moving up the Rappahannock.

Beginning in late April, Hooker marched the bulk of his army up the river. With admirable speed, his corps commanders got more than 70,000 men across several fords and moving smartly against the flank and rear of Lee's 40,000 men. But soon, in a monumental failure of nerve, Hooker drew back and went on the defensive around the crossroads of Chancellorsville. This was all Lee and Stonewall Jackson needed. Sending Jackson on a daring flank march, Lee contrived a battle considered his masterpiece. He so confounded Hooker that in three days the Federal army was speeding back across the Rappahannock. Lincoln had urged the boastful Hooker to "give us victories." Instead, he had delivered another ignominious defeat.

For Lee, however, the victory was sadly tainted by the loss of Jackson, who was mortally wounded by his pickets on the night after the great flank march. Lee lamented that he had lost his right arm.

MAJ. GEN. JOSEPH HOOKER

Hooker began his march around Lee's army by sending the corps of George Meade, Oliver Howard, and Henry Slocum northeast to cross the Rappahannock at Kelly's Ford on April 29. The three corps then crossed the Rapidan at Germanna and Ely's fords and turned southeast to converge on the crossroads called Chancellorsville. Hooker also ordered the corps of Darius Couch and Daniel Sickles to cross the Rappahannock at United States Ford and join the main force. In the meantime, John Sedgwick would lead his own VI Corps and John Reynolds' I Corps in a feigned attack south of Fredericksburg. Lee, slow to see the Federal threat, first sent only Richard Anderson's division west on the 29th, but soon dispatched Jackson with most of the Confederate army in the same direction. He left only Jubal Early's division and a brigade of Lafayette McLaws to guard Fredericksburg.

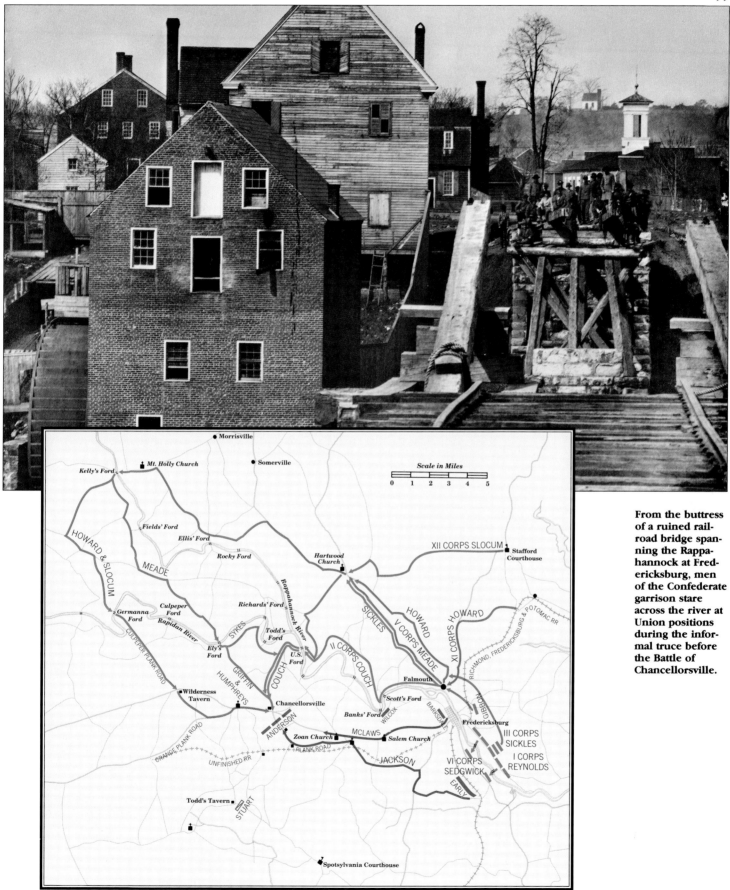

From the buttress of a ruined railroad bridge spanning the Rappahannock at Fredericksburg, men of the Confederate garrison stare across the river at Union positions during the informal truce before the Battle of Chancellorsville.

ORDER OF BATTLE

ARMY OF NORTHERN VIRGINIA
LEE
58,900 MEN

FIRST CORPS (LESS TWO DIVISIONS)
LONGSTREET (ABSENT)

McLAWS' DIVISION
WOFFORD'S BRIGADE
KERSHAW'S BRIGADE
SEMMES' BRIGADE
BARKSDALE'S BRIGADE

ANDERSON'S DIVISION
WILCOX'S BRIGADE
MAHONE'S BRIGADE
WRIGHT'S BRIGADE
POSEY'S BRIGADE
PERRY'S BRIGADE

SECOND CORPS
JACKSON

A. P. HILL'S DIVISION
HETH'S BRIGADE
McGOWAN'S BRIGADE
THOMAS' BRIGADE
ARCHER'S BRIGADE
LANE'S BRIGADE
PENDER'S BRIGADE

RODES' DIVISION
RODES' BRIGADE
DOLE'S BRIGADE
COLQUITT'S BRIGADE
IVERSON'S BRIGADE
RAMSEUR'S BRIGADE

EARLY'S DIVISION
GORDON'S BRIGADE
SMITH'S BRIGADE
HOKE'S BRIGADE
HAYS' BRIGADE

COLSTON'S DIVISION
PAXTON'S BRIGADE
WARREN'S BRIGADE
J. R. JONES' BRIGADE
NICHOLLS' BRIGADE

CAVALRY
STUART

HAMPTON'S BRIGADE
F. LEE'S BRIGADE

W. H. F. LEE'S BRIGADE
W. E. JONES' BRIGADE

ARMY OF THE POTOMAC
HOOKER
134,600 MEN

I CORPS REYNOLDS

FIRST DIVISION: WADSWORTH
Brigades: PHELPS, CUTLER, PAUL, MEREDITH

SECOND DIVISION: ROBINSON
Brigades: ROOT, BAXTER, LEONARD

THIRD DIVISION: DOUBLEDAY
Brigades: ROWLEY, STONE

V CORPS MEADE

FIRST DIVISION: GRIFFIN
Brigades: BARNES, McQUADE, STOCKTON

SECOND DIVISION: SYKES
Brigades: AYRES, BURBANK, O'RORKE

THIRD DIVISION: HUMPHREYS
Brigades: TYLER, ALLABACH

II CORPS COUCH

FIRST DIVISION: HANCOCK
Brigades: CALDWELL, MEAGHER, ZOOK, BROOKE

SECOND DIVISION: GIBBON
Brigades: SULLY, OWEN, HALL

THIRD DIVISION: FRENCH
Brigades: CARROLL, HAYS, MacGREGOR

VI CORPS SEDGWICK

FIRST DIVISION: BROOKS
Brigades: BROWN, BARTLETT, RUSSELL

SECOND DIVISION: HOWE
Brigades: GRANT, NEILL

THIRD DIVISION: NEWTON
Brigades: SHALER, BROWNE, WHEATON

XII CORPS SLOCUM

FIRST DIVISION: WILLIAMS
Brigades: KNIPE, ROSS, RUGER

SECOND DIVISION: GEARY
Brigades: CANDY, KANE, GREENE

III CORPS SICKLES

FIRST DIVISION: BIRNEY
Brigades: GRAHAM, WARD, HAYMAN

SECOND DIVISION: BERRY
Brigades: CARR, REVERE, MOTT

THIRD DIVISION: WHIPPLE
Brigades: FRANKLIN, BOWMAN, BERDAN

XI CORPS HOWARD

FIRST DIVISION: DEVENS
Brigades: VON GILSA, McLEAN

SECOND DIVISION: VON STEINWEHR
Brigades: BUSCHBECK, BARLOW

THIRD DIVISION: SCHURZ
Brigades: SCHIMMELFENNIG, KRZYZANOWSKI

CAVALRY
STONEMAN

FIRST DIVISION: PLEASONTON
Brigades: DAVIS, DEVIN

SECOND DIVISION: AVERELL
Brigades: SARGENT, McINTOSH

THIRD DIVISION: GREGG
Brigades: KILPATRICK, WYNDHAM

Seated on hardtack boxes in the woods near Chancellorsville, Generals Lee *(left)* and Jackson quietly make plans to divide their forces and attack Hooker's Federals. Lee holds a map, sketched by Jackson's topographical expert Jedediah Hotchkiss, that charted the concealed route to the enemy's uncovered right flank. After learning that the Federal left and center were largely unassailable, Lee gave his approval to Jackson's bold proposal.

JACKSON'S FLANK MARCH AND ATTACK, MAY 2

In one of the great gambles of the war, Jackson set out on the morning of May 2 with the bulk of the Confederate force, about 26,000 men, on a furtive 14-mile march around the Federal right, leaving Lee with only 14,000 men to face Hooker's 70,000. The Federals spotted rear elements of Jackson's column passing an ironworks called Catherine Furnace, and two divisions of Sickles' III Corps attacked. Regiments from Anderson's and A. P. Hill's divisions threw the Federals back. Other Union officers also saw parts of Jackson's column along Brock Road toward the Orange Plank Road, but their warnings were ignored by Hooker, who by midday was convinced Lee was retreating. After nine hours of marching, Jackson deployed his troops in three lines perpendicular to the Turnpike and extending a mile on either side of it. At 5:00 p.m., the Confederates, with Robert Rodes' division leading, stormed over the Federal pickets and within half an hour had routed Howard's unprepared XI Corps.

102

Brigadier General Robert Rodes, recovered from a thigh wound received at Antietam and now commanding a Confederate division, led the initial drive on Howard's corps. Howard, who had refused to believe an attack was imminent, later wrote that Rodes' assault was like "a terrible gale" with "quick lightning from a hundred points at once."

A brigade of Rodes' division, shouting the Rebel yell, storms a Federal breastworks on the Turnpike west of Chancellorsville, taking Union defenders by surprise. Only a handful of regiments managed to get off a few volleys before giving way. Echoes of the Confederate troops' wild scream, wrote a survivor of the battle, "swept the country for miles."

A Union officer brandishing pistol and saber *(right)* tries in vain to slow the stampede of the XI Corps down the Plank Road. The photograph below shows a stretch of the partially planked track where it met a side lane *(background)* down which Stonewall Jackson was riding when he was accidentally shot by Rebel pickets.

104

A fanciful painting of the Chancellorsville battle at sunset on May 2 shows the red brick Chancellor House at the intersection of the turnpike and Plank Road. Nearby, Federal infantry and artillery try to form a defensive perimeter while cavalrymen ride down the Plank Road to try to slow the oncoming enemy. Jackson's initial Confederate attack came out of the woods of the Wilderness to the west at upper left. In the foreground at right, Lee's troops charge from the southeast, an attack that actually came the next day.

LT. GEN. JAMES EWELL BROWN "JEB" STUART

STUART'S ATTACK, MAY 3

During the night of May 2-3, the Federals frantically reorganized their lines, forming a loop around the Chancellor House with two wings extending northward in a crude V toward the Rappahannock. Jeb Stuart, who had assumed command after Jackson was wounded, sent his men forward at first light, with William Dorsey Pender's brigade of Henry Heth's division driving into the Federal perimeter from the west. The crucial moment came when James Archer's brigade charged virtually unopposed up the slopes of a key hill called Hazel Grove, abandoned by Sickles' men on the orders of Hooker, who thought the position too exposed. Colonel E. Porter Alexander immediately rushed 30 guns onto the knoll and began pouring a murderous fire on the brigades of Slocum's XII Corps and Sickles' III Corps. Soon Stuart renewed his attack while Lee began to close in from the southeast. By noon the Federal position had become untenable, and Hooker ordered his army to fall back to new positions north of Chancellorsville.

Winfield Scott Hancock, given command of the Federal rear guard, delayed the enemy pursuit with skill, allowing his corps commander, Darius Couch, to organize a defensive perimeter.

E. Porter Alexander, the brilliant Confederate artillerist, managed in the morning of May 3 to assemble the guns that whipsawed the Federal lines from Hazel Grove. He was credited by Lee with "the successful issue of the contest."

A Federal battle line covering the gradual retreat of Hooker's army from Chancellorsville bravely holds off attacks by the pursuing Confederates. Three of Hooker's subordinates, Meade, Reynolds, and Howard, wanted to fight it out south of the Rappahannock and even use the still-powerful Federal force to take the offensive, but Hooker ordered the entire army to withdraw.

Brigadier General Herman Haupt *(left)*, field commander of U.S. military railroads, and an assistant survey wrecked Confederate caissons and dead horses on Marye's Heights at the Fredericksburg battlefield after Sedgwick's May 3 attack.

During the withdrawal of the Federal VI Corps to the Rappahannock on May 4, troops of the Vermont Brigade, part of Albion Howe's division, successfully held off Jubal Early's oncoming Confederates. Protecting the Federal left, Howe's stout defense enabled Sedgwick's corps to recross the river at Scott's Ford.

SALEM CHURCH/FEDERAL RETREAT, MAY 3-5

On the morning of May 3, Sedgwick, ordered by Hooker to march his 23,000 men to join the main Federal force, sent the divisions of John Gibbon and John Newton advancing by the most direct route westward from Fredericksburg—straight up Marye's Heights. As in December, the fighting was desperate and bloody, but in a final rush the Federals took the stone wall, sending Jubal Early's outnumbered defenders fleeing southward. That afternoon, however, Sedgwick's men, reaching Salem Church on the Turnpike, were brought to a standstill by Lafayette McLaws' division. The next day Lee put in action a plan to annihilate Sedgwick's corps, bringing up artillery to support a three-pronged attack by McLaws, Richard Anderson, and Early, who had marched back into action. But through a combination of Confederate errors and a skillfully executed withdrawal, Sedgwick slipped out of the trap and during the night of May 4-5 got his force across the Rappahannock at Scott's Ford. By the morning of May 6, the six Federal corps north of Chancellorsville had also crossed, pressed by Stuart's force—which at 25,000 men was one-third of the fleeing Union army.

GETTYSBURG CAMPAIGN

Only days after his triumph at Chancellorsville, Robert E. Lee decided again to head for the rich farmlands of Pennsylvania. Lee intended to force the Army of the Potomac to engage him in a campaign of maneuver, the kind of war that afforded his outnumbered army its best hope of victory. At the same time, a successful invasion would surely encourage the North's Peace Democrats to demand an end to the fighting—with a treaty favorable to the South. It might also induce Britain and France to recognize the Confederacy and possibly intervene on its behalf.

Starting early in June 1863, Lee began slipping his army northwest toward the Shenandoah Valley. First to move were Jeb Stuart's horsemen, who soon became embroiled in a battle with Federal cavalry *(next two pages).* Then came Stonewall Jackson's 2d Corps, now led by Richard Ewell, who had largely recovered from the loss of a leg at Second Manassas. Ewell quickly crossed the Blue Ridge into the Shenandoah and, trouncing a Federal force at Winchester, sped down the Valley. Next came Longstreet and his corps, followed by the newly created 3d Corps under A. P. Hill. Fording the Potomac, all three corps entered the Cumberland Valley—and immediately sent out foraging parties to scour the countryside. Elements of Ewell's corps reached the Susquehanna River; a cavalry detachment camped four miles from the Pennsylvania capital of Harrisburg.

On June 29, Lee sent urgent messages ordering all units to concentrate in the vicinity of Gettysburg to face the Federal army that had moved northward in pursuit with surprising swiftness. There, beginning on July 1, more than 160,000 Americans would fight a three-day battle that for its violence—and its importance—would forever be etched in the national memory. When silence fell over the Pennsylvania ridges and fields on July 3, Lee's cause had passed its high tide, and Confederate hopes had begun to fade.

Confederate troops, their trousers rolled, wade across the upper Potomac on their way to Pennsylvania.

After shifting his army west to Culpeper, Lee *(red lines)* marched through three gaps in the Blue Ridge and proceeded north, screened by the mountains. Once across the Potomac, his corps fanned out into the rich farmlands of the Cumberland Valley. On June 13, General Hooker started the Union army north on parallel routes *(blue lines)* from Fredericksburg through Northern Virginia and into Maryland. There General George Meade replaced Hooker and quickly hurried his new command into Pennsylvania to find and intercept Lee. Meanwhile, Jeb Stuart took three brigades of cavalry on a foray *(broken red lines)* that circled the Federal army—but left Lee without the scouts he needed to track Union movements.

PENNSYLVANIA

Scale in Miles

0 5 10 20 30 40

Harrisburg

Mechanicsburg

Carlisle

Breeches Creek

Mount Holly Springs

Yellow

PENNSYLVANIA RR

Wrightsville

Columbia

Shippensburg

Petersburg

Dover

York

McConnellsburg

Chambersburg

Middletown

Heidlersburg

Abbotstown

New Oxford

Mercersburg

Cashtown

Greencastle

Gettysburg

Hanover

Littlestown

Waynesboro

Emmitsburg

Creek

Union Mills

Hagerstown

Taneytown

Westminster

Williamsport

Union Bridge

Boonsboro

Sharpsburg

Frederick

Mount Airy

Shepherdstown

Martinsburg

Berlin

Baltimore

Bunker Hill

Harpers Ferry

Urbana

Hyattstown

Stephenson's Depot

Summit Point

Barnesville

Clarksburg

MARYLAND

Winchester

Berryville

Poolesville

Leesburg

Rockville

Strasburg

Upperville

Aldie

Dranesville

Washington, D.C.

Middleburg

Gum Springs

Front Royal

Salem

Centreville

Falls Church

Fairfax Court House

Alexandria

Chester Gap

Manassas Junction

VIRGINIA

Warrenton

Sperryville

Bealeton

Dumfries

Brandy Station

Culpeper Court House

Stafford Court House

Aquia

Madison Court House

Falmouth

Chancellorsville

Fredericksburg

RICHMOND

Orange Court House

Spotsylvania Court House

Potomac River

Rappahannock River

A few days after Hooker got wind of Lee's shift westward, he learned further that Jeb Stuart's cavalry was concentrated near Culpeper. Hooker ordered his own troopers, now massed in one large corps led by Brig. Gen. Alfred Pleasonton, to locate and attack Lee's horsemen. Early on June 9, after determining that the Confederates were camped near a hamlet called Brandy Station, Pleasonton sent Gen. John Buford's division across the Rappahannock to attack the northern end of the Confederate position. Buford's horsemen nearly broke through Wade Hampton's hastily improvised defenses in savage hand-to-hand fighting. Meanwhile, two divisions under David Gregg and Alfred Duffié circled via Kelly's Ford and hit Stuart in the right flank and rear. Duffié was slow in attacking, but Gregg's brigades under Hugh Judson Kilpatrick and the Englishman Sir Percy Wyndham cut their way into Stuart's main force east of Brandy Station. The Confederate defenses stiffened, and, by early evening, Pleasonton was forced to pull his various units back. But the Federal cavalrymen had given the vaunted Stuart a bad day. By holding their own in the War's largest all-cavalry battle, the Union horsemen had gained a new confidence that would last through the War.

In Buford's final attack, the 2d U.S. Cavalry gallops past two retiring Federal units toward W. H. F. Lee's Confederates on the rise in the distance.

ORDER OF BATTLE
ARMY OF NORTHERN VIRGINIA
LEE
75,000 MEN

FIRST CORPS
LONGSTREET

McLAWS' DIVISION	**PICKETT'S DIVISION**	**HOOD'S DIVISION**
KERSHAW'S BRIGADE	GARNETT'S BRIGADE	LAW'S BRIGADE
SEMMES' BRIGADE	KEMPER'S BRIGADE	ROBERTSON'S BRIGADE
BARKSDALE'S BRIGADE	ARMISTEAD'S BRIGADE	G. T. ANDERSON'S BRIGADE
WOFFORD'S BRIGADE		BENNING'S BRIGADE

SECOND CORPS
EWELL

EARLY'S DIVISION	**JOHNSON'S DIVISION**	**RODES' DIVISION**
HAYS' BRIGADE	STEUART'S BRIGADE	DANIEL'S BRIGADE
SMITH'S BRIGADE	WALKER'S BRIGADE	IVERSON'S BRIGADE
GORDON'S BRIGADE	WILLIAMS' BRIGADE	DOLES' BRIGADE
AVERY'S BRIGADE	JONES' BRIGADE	RAMSEUR'S BRIGADE
		O'NEAL'S BRIGADE

THIRD CORPS
HILL

R. H. ANDERSON'S DIVISION	**HETH'S DIVISION**	**PENDER'S DIVISION**
WILCOX'S BRIGADE	PETTIGREW'S BRIGADE	PERRIN'S BRIGADE
WRIGHT'S BRIGADE	BROCKENBROUGH'S BRIGADE	LANE'S BRIGADE
MAHONE'S BRIGADE	ARCHER'S BRIGADE	THOMAS' BRIGADE
LANG'S BRIGADE	DAVIS' BRIGADE	SCALES' BRIGADE
POSEY'S BRIGADE		

CAVALRY
STUART

HAMPTON'S BRIGADE
F. LEE'S BRIGADE
ROBERTSON'S BRIGADE
JENKINS' BRIGADE
JONES' BRIGADE
W. H. F. LEE'S BRIGADE

ARMY OF THE POTOMAC
MEADE
85,500 MEN

I CORPS REYNOLDS

FIRST DIVISION: WADSWORTH
Brigades: MEREDITH, CUTLER

SECOND DIVISION: ROBINSON
Brigades: PAUL, BAXTER

THIRD DIVISION: ROWLEY
Brigades: BIDDLE, STONE, STANNARD

II CORPS HANCOCK

FIRST DIVISION: CALDWELL
Brigades: CROSS, KELLY, ZOOK, BROOKE

SECOND DIVISION: GIBBON
Brigades: HARROW, WEBB, HALL

THIRD DIVISION: HAYS
Brigades: CARROLL, SMYTH, WILLARD

III CORPS SICKLES

FIRST DIVISION: BIRNEY
Brigades: GRAHAM, WARD, DE TROBRIAND

SECOND DIVISION: HUMPHREYS
Brigades: CARR, BREWSTER, BURLING

V CORPS SYKES

FIRST DIVISION: BARNES
Brigades: TILTON, SWEITZER, VINCENT

SECOND DIVISION: AYRES
Brigades: DAY, BURBANK, WEED

THIRD DIVISION: CRAWFORD
Brigades: McCANDLESS, FISHER

VI CORPS SEDGWICK

FIRST DIVISION: WRIGHT
Brigades: TORBERT, BARTLETT, RUSSELL

SECOND DIVISION: HOWE
Brigades: GRANT, NEILL

THIRD DIVISION: NEWTON
Brigades: SHALER, EUSTIS, WHEATON

XI CORPS HOWARD

FIRST DIVISION: BARLOW
Brigades: VON GILSA, AMES

SECOND DIVISION: VON STEINWEHR
Brigades: COSTER, SMITH

THIRD DIVISION: SCHURZ
Brigades: SCHIMMELFENNIG, KRZYZANOWSKI

XII CORPS SLOCUM

FIRST DIVISION: WILLIAMS
Brigades: McDOUGALL, LOCKWOOD, RUGER

SECOND DIVISION: GEARY
Brigades: CANDY, COBHAM, GREENE

CAVALRY CORPS PLEASONTON

FIRST DIVISION: BUFORD
Brigades: GAMBLE, DEVIN, MERRITT

SECOND DIVISION: GREGG
Brigades: McINTOSH, HUEY, GREGG

THIRD DIVISION: KILPATRICK
Brigades: FARNSWORTH, CUSTER

At the height of his reputation in the summer of 1863, Robert E. Lee was beloved by his countrymen, feared by his enemies, and respected by both. His careworn, grandfatherly face disguised the grim determination and fierce combativeness that for a second time compelled him to carry the War north.

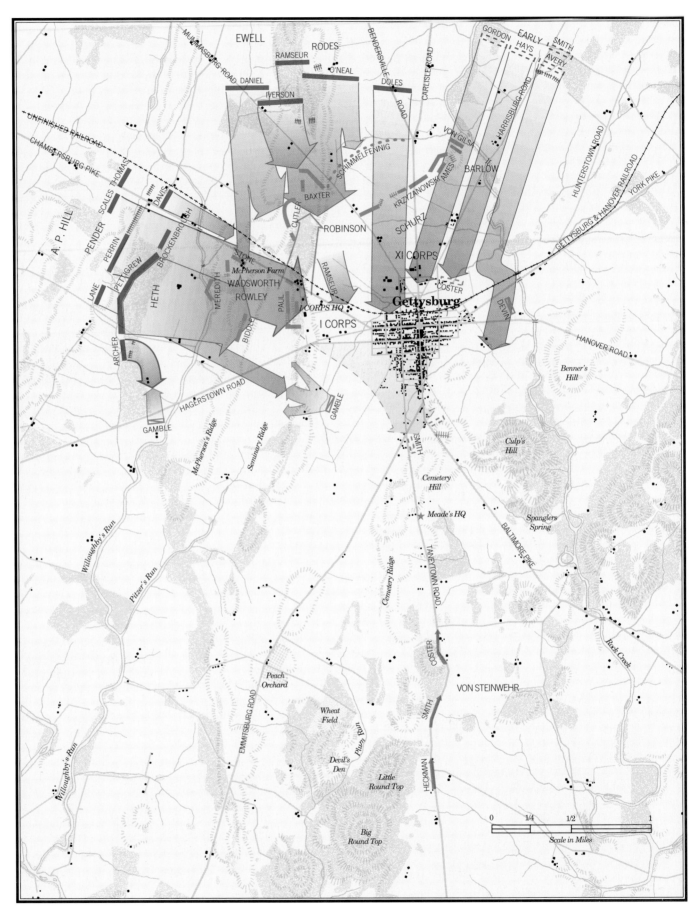

EWELL

RODES

RAMSEUR

O'NEAL

DANIEL

IVERSON

DOLES

BENDERSVILLE ROAD

CARLISLE ROAD

GORDON EARLY SMITH

HAYS

AVERY

HARRISBURG ROAD

VON GILSA

SCHIMMELFENNIG

BARLOW

AMES

KRZYZANOWSKI

SCHURZ

XI CORPS

UNFINISHED RAILROAD

CHAMBERSBURG PIKE

THOMAS

SCALES

DAVIS

A. P. HILL

PENDER

PERRIN

BROCKENBROUGH

CUTLER

BAXTER

ROBINSON

RAMSEUR

HUNTERSTOWN ROAD

GETTYSBURG & HANOVER RAILROAD

YORK PIKE

LANE

PETTIGREW

STONE

McPherson Farm

MEREDITH

WADSWORTH

ROWLEY

PAUL

I CORPS HQ

COSTER

DEVIN

HETH

BIDDLE

Gettysburg

I CORPS

HANOVER ROAD

ARCHER

HAGERSTOWN ROAD

GAMBLE

Benner's Hill

GAMBLE

McPherson's Ridge

Seminary Ridge

SMITH

Culp's Hill

Cemetery Hill

Spanglers Spring

Willoughby's Run

Pitzer's Run

Meade's HQ

Cemetery Ridge

TANEYTOWN ROAD

BALTIMORE PIKE

Rock Creek

COSTER

Peach Orchard

SMITH

VON STEINWEHR

Emmitsburg Road

Willoughby's Run

Wheat Field

Plum Run

Devil's Den

Little Round Top

HECKMAN

Big Round Top

0   1/4   1/2   1

Scale in Miles

MUMMASBURG ROAD

CHAMBERSBURG PIKE

UNFINISHED RAILROAD

Seminary Ridge

CARLISLE ROAD

HARRISBURG ROAD

HUNTERSTOWN ROAD

GETTYSBURG & HANOVER RAILROAD

YORK PIKE

HETH

Lee's HQ

O'NEAL

DANIEL

Lutheran Seminary

RODES

EWELL

Gettysburg

GORDON

EARLY

HAYS

AVERY

WILLIAMS

JOHNSON

STEUART

WALKER

HANOVER ROAD

Benner's Hill

JONES

RAMSEUR

IVERSON

DOLES

PENDER

SCALES

PERRIN

MAHONE

LANE

THOMAS

A. P. HILL

ANDERSON

POSEY

WRIGHT

LANG

HAGERSTOWN ROAD

SCHURZ

AMES

XI CORPS

VON STEINWEHR

Cemetery Hill

WADSWORTH

GEARY

GREEN

Culp's Hill

XII CORPS

RUGER

KANE

Bliss House

I CORPS

DOUBLEDAY

HAYS

WEBB

Meade's HQ

II CORPS

GIBBON

BALTIMORE PIKE

Codori House

HARROW

WILCOX

HUMPHREYS

BROOKE

ZOOK

CROSS

KELLY

CALDWELL

Cemetery Ridge

BARNES

CRAWFORD

Willoughby's Run

Pitzer's Run

BREWSTER

III CORPS

SICKLES

Sherfy House

BIRNEY

Trostle House

Artillery Reserve

AYRES

V CORPS

WOFFORD

BARKSDALE

GRAHAM

Peach Orchard

DE TROBRIAND

VI CORPS

MCLAWS

SEMMES

KERSHAW

EMMITSBURG ROAD

Wheat Field

WARD

Devil's Den

Rock Creek

LONGSTREET

HOOD

ANDERSON

ROBERTSON

BENNING

LAW

Plum Run

Little Round Top

TANEYTOWN ROAD

Big Round Top

0   1/4   1/2   1

Scale in Miles

120

John Bell Hood, a Kentucky-born West Pointer, was an implacable warrior who had led his famed Texas brigade in the fighting at the Seven Days' Battles, Second Bull Run, and Antietam. A division commander at Gettysburg, he was severely wounded early in the fighting on July 2 and replaced by Evander Law. Hood had, said one contemporary, "a sad Quixote face, the face of an old crusader."

Troops of Ward's Federal brigade begin to give way as Hood's Confederates scramble into the Devil's Den, a labyrinth of huge boulders and rock-walled passages. Ward lost one-third of the men in his brigade of New York, Pennsylvania, Indiana, and Maine regiments, but his troops inflicted heavy losses on the attacking Rebels.

ROUND TOP—DEVIL'S DEN, FIRST PHASE

Longstreet's attack against the Federal left got under way around 4:00 p.m. when Hood sent Law's and part of Robertson's brigades toward Big Round Top and Plum Run Valley. Encountering only light fire from skirmishers and a single artillery battery, the Confederates easily reached the entrance to the valley and the summit of Big Round Top. But when they pushed on toward Little Round Top, they were stopped by Vincent's Federal brigade, dispatched to the hill at the last minute by General Meade's chief engineer, Gouverneur Warren. Meanwhile, the rest of Robertson's brigade, along with Anderson's and Benning's Georgia brigades, advanced into Plum Run Valley from the west and quickly found themselves in a bloody fight for the boulder-strewn cul-de-sac dubbed the Devil's Den. There the Confederates finally hammered back Ward's Federal brigade, which was trying to hold the left flank of Sickles' exposed III Corps.

After the battle, the rock-strewn Plum Run Valley was soon to become known as the Valley of Death. In the background are the humps of Big Round Top on the right, Little Round Top on the left.

ROUND TOP—DEVIL'S DEN, SECOND PHASE

Attacking up the saddle between Big Round Top and Little Round Top, Alabamians and Texans of Robertson's and Law's brigades repeatedly charged the Federal line on Little Round Top through the waning hours of July 2. Several times they almost broke through, but were stopped by murderous Federal fire and desperate local counterattacks by Vincent's and Weed's brigades. Meanwhile, Benning's Georgians held their hard-won ground around the Devil's Den while Anderson's troops wheeled north to support McLaw's attack into the Wheat Field.

Col. Joshua Chamberlain left a professorship at Maine's Bowdoin College to serve in the Union army, eventually taking command of the 20th Maine. His bold counterattack on Little Round Top won him the Medal of Honor.

Parrott guns of Lt. Charles Hazlett's Battery D, 5th U.S. Artillery, fire from their commanding position on the summit of Little Round Top.

Dashing down the south slope of Little Round Top, the 20th Maine, led by Col. Joshua Chamberlain *(sword raised, right of center),* attacks the 15th Alabama under Col. William Oates *(right foreground),* who tries to rally his men. Chamberlain ordered the bayonet attack as a last resort after his men had run out of ammunition.

Dozens of Confederate dead, probably killed by Union fire from Little Round Top, can be seen sprawled amid the open rocky area east of Plum Run and the Devil's Den that came to be known as the Slaughter Pen.

MAJ. GEN. DANIEL E. SICKLES

WHEAT FIELD—PEACH ORCHARD, FIRST PHASE

In late afternoon, Anderson's brigade on Hood's left drove back the left wing of Sickles' III Corps, then slammed into Caldwell's division from the II Corps that had moved up into the Wheat Field. Around 5:30, just as Anderson was forced to fall back, Longstreet ordered McLaws' division into the fight, with Kershaw's brigade first and Semmes' brigade following. After taking heavy fire from Federal artillery on their left flank, McLaws' men engaged elements of three Federal divisions in a vicious seesaw battle for control of the Wheat Field, which changed hands six times.

General Sickles *(center)* gallops to inspect Federal troops waiting near the Peach Orchard *(right)* for Confederates to attack from the distant trees.

MAJ. GEN. LAFAYETTE McLAWS

WHEAT FIELD—PEACH ORCHARD, SECOND PHASE

While the fighting raged on in the Wheat Field, McLaws launched the brigades of Barksdale and Wofford against Graham's brigade, which held the apex of Sickles' salient at the Peach Orchard. The Federals were swept away in a matter of minutes, and soon the whole Union line gave way in a general retreat back across Plum Run. But after a final attack to the north by elements of A. P. Hill's corps, the Confederates' ground assault sputtered to a halt in the face of darkness, mounting casualties, and stiffening Federal resistance on Cemetery Ridge.

Union dead, probably from Sickles' III Corps, litter a trampled meadow as a burial detail gathers in the distance. The bodies are without shoes, indicating that the Confederates who held the area after the fighting on July 2 had scavenged equipment from the dead.

Urged on by Col. William Colvill *(with arm upraised at center),* troops of the 1st Minnesota make a headlong countercharge into Cadmus Wilcox's Confederates near Cemetery Ridge. Wilcox, exploiting a gap left in the Federal III Corps line during the confused fighting in the Wheat Field and Peach Orchard, threatened momentarily to crack the main Union defenses. Colvill's Minnesotans threw the Confederates back—at a cost of 82 percent of the regiment's men.

General Samuel Crawford's Pennsylvania Reserve Division charges across Plum Run Valley and into Longstreet's Confederates, who had paused on the valley's western side after chasing the last of the Federals from the Wheat Field. Crawford's assault was one of several local Federal counterattacks launched at dusk that checked the advance of the exhausted Rebels.

128

CULP'S HILL—CEMETERY HILL

Lacking precise orders from Lee and displaying little initiative, Richard Ewell failed to attack the northern end of the Federal line until around 6:30 p.m. His twilight assaults, however, threatened to overwhelm the Union defenses. Moving against Culp's Hill from the east, the brigades of Steuart, Jones, and Williams clawed their way to the summit, only to be stopped by Greene's Federals firing from behind hastily erected but formidable breastworks. Attacking from the north, around 8:00 p.m., Hays' Louisiana brigade and Avery's North Carolinians routed a line of Federals behind a stone wall, burst over the brow of Cemetery Hill, drove back still more defenders, and swarmed into the forwardmost Union artillery positions. But the Rebels, now disorganized, shot up, and fighting in pitch darkness, were driven back down the hill by Federal counterattacks spearheaded by Carroll's and Schurz's brigades. The next morning, Ewell renewed his attacks against Culp's Hill only to be repulsed a second time.

Taking cover behind boulders and trees, Confederates of J. M. Williams' brigade advance up Culp's Hill toward Federal positions on the summit.

129

A postbattle photograph taken from the position of the 5th Maine Battery on Stevens Hill shows the ground crossed by Avery's brigade during its attack on Cemetery Hill *(left)*. The battery's six 12-pounders tore huge gaps in the North Carolinians' ranks as they advanced from right to left across the field of view.

Troops of Hays' 9th Louisiana charge the battery of Capt. R. Bruce Ricketts on the crest of Cemetery Hill. The Louisiana Tigers nearly overran Ricketts' guns before they were forced to retreat.

**BRIG. GEN.
HARRY THOMPSON HAYS**

131

George Pickett, who lost 3,000 men in the doomed charge, uttered a simple but moving epitaph when asked to prepare his division for a Federal countercharge. "General Lee," he said, "I have no division now."

Brig. Gen. James Johnston Pettigrew, commanding Heth's division, was wounded during the charge but was one of the last to leave the field. Two weeks later he was killed during the retreat from Gettysburg.

PICKETT'S CHARGE, JULY 3

After two days of fighting, the Confederates retained the initiative, but the costly attacks against the Federal flanks had failed to dislodge Meade's army. Still grimly determined to force the issue at Gettysburg, Lee deployed his forces on the third day, this time on the weakened center of the Union line *(map, left)*. Making the attack would be the fresh troops of General George Pickett's division along with already battered units from Hill's corps, including the wounded Henry Heth's division, now led by James Pettigrew, plus two of Pender's brigades under Isaac Trimble. Facing the Confederates on Cemetery Ridge were elements of the I and II Corps under Hancock's command with reserves posted nearby. After a two-hour artillery bombardment that inflicted little damage on the Federal front line, the Confederate infantry started forward at 3:00 p.m. *(map,*

above). The brigades of James Kemper, Richard Garnett, and Lewis Armistead advanced obliquely to their left to close up with Pettigrew, exposing their right flanks to fire from Union guns. Pettigrew's men were similarly mauled by batteries on Cemetery Hill. As the flanks of both divisions contracted, the Federals overlapped the Confederates and poured in a terrible fire. Despite dreadful losses, Pettigrew's men rushed the Federal line defended by Hays' division—and were staggered by musket and cannon fire. Most of the survivors of Pickett's brigades attacked the Angle, a jog in a stone wall, where they were pulverized by fire from Gibbon's division. The Rebels flooded over the wall but were blasted back by Union reserves. With that repulse, the Confederates began streaming to the rear. The charge—and the Battle of Gettysburg—was over.

The painting below portrays the climactic moment when the Confederates, now led by Lewis Armistead, the last of Pickett's brigadier generals still on his feet, swarmed over the wall near the Angle. They were met by murderous fire from Federal reinforcements, who then charged and hurled back the attackers. As the battered survivors staggered back to Seminary Ridge, Lee rode among them *(right)* offering encouragement and accepting the blame for the failure of the attack. The next evening he set his army in motion toward Virginia, starting a painful 10-day retreat during which he managed to hold off Meade's delayed, ineffective pursuit and withdraw his forces across the Potomac River. Lee's losses at Gettysburg were catastrophic: about 28,000 men, or nearly 40 percent of his force, compared with about 25 percent for the Federals. But Lee's army had survived to fight again.

WILDERNESS CAMPAIGN

On March 8, 1864, a journalist attending a White House reception for Ulysses S. Grant described the heralded honoree as a "little, scared-looking man." When the unassuming lieutenant general took command of all Union forces four days later, his troops were similarly unimpressed. President Lincoln, however, knew Grant for a fighter and was convinced he would achieve what a succession of Union generals had not—the destruction of the Confederate armies and the conquest of the Confederacy. The president's confidence would be put to the test that spring as his new commander led the Union forces against the army of the formidable and brilliant Robert E. Lee in a series of battles whose names would live in history: the Wilderness, Spotsylvania, and Cold Harbor.

Grant reorganized and reequipped the Army of the Potomac, which awaited the coming Wilderness campaign in winter quarters at Brandy Station, Virginia, and reinforced its ranks with idle troops from Washington and other garrisons. His orders to General George Meade, commander of the Army of the Potomac, were succinct:

In the opening move of the Federal offensive in the Wilderness, troops of Gen. John Sedgwick's VI Corps cross a pontoon bridge over the Rapidan River at Germanna Ford on May 4.

"Lee's army will be your objective point. Wherever Lee goes, there you will go also." General Grant would map the strategy and General Meade the tactics in a series of flanking maneuvers that would culminate in a climactic drive on Richmond.

Blocking the path to the Confederate capital was Lee's Army of Northern Virginia, which had pulled back south of the Rapidan River after being defeated at Gettysburg the year before. Heavy casualties and a rash of desertions had sapped the strength of the Rebels, and the South, with its smaller population, was hard-pressed to replace the losses.

Counting on the Union's superior reserves of men and matériel, Grant was confident that he could defeat Lee's forces by grinding them down in a war of attrition. In the spring of 1864, as the nation entered the final and most bitter year of the Civil War, Grant crossed the Rapidan and met his adversary in the tangled thickets of the Wilderness. In the series of close-range, bloody battles that followed, the new commander learned that there would be no easy victories.

Jubal Early returned to the Valley in mid-June with orders from Lee to clear it of Federal forces in time for the harvest, and, if possible, to strike northward and force Grant to loosen his grip on Richmond and Petersburg. Early commanded an underfed, tattered corps, numbering barely 8,000 men. But many were seasoned Valley campaigners who had marched with Stonewall Jackson two years before.

Lexington citizens go about their daily business on the town's main street after a three-day Federal occupation. Union soldiers reduced the Virginia Military Institute *(on the horizon)* to ruins, and destroyed all the food and supplies they could not carry off.

Lew Wallace estimated that his improvised army was "probably too small to defeat the Confederates at Monocacy" but strong enough to gain time. "I made up my mind to fight."

Infantrymen of the 10th Vermont retreat gingerly over the railroad bridge across the Monocacy River near the end of the daylong battle. In a show of chivalry that was rare this late in the War, the Confederate artillery held its fire while the Union soldiers crossed the open span.

Union artillerymen prepare for drill inside Fort Stevens, where Jubal Early's offensive ended after two days four miles from the White House. The fort's "position was naturally strong," Early wrote, "and every possible approach was raked by artillery."

In the first major engagement of his invasion of the North, Jubal Early faced Lew Wallace on July 9 at Monocacy Junction, 45 miles west of Baltimore. Here, where a B & O railroad bridge crossed the Monocacy River, Wallace had determined to delay Early's advance on Washington. Early's Confederates found Wallace's smaller force of Federals entrenched behind the river. At noon, as Rodes threatened the Federal right about two miles north of the bridge and Ramseur pressed the Federal skirmish line defending Monocacy Junction, Gordon's division crossed the river and attacked the Union left. Gordon drove back Ricketts' VI Corps division, forcing Wallace to retreat toward Baltimore. At a cost of 1,294 casualties, he had won 24 hours for the assembly of defenses at the Federal capital and had cost Early some 700 men. After his defeat, Wallace was stripped of his Middle Department command. But he was soon reinstated by Grant, who noted that in defeat, Wallace had given more service to the Federal cause than many commanders rendered in victory.

On August 7, 1864, Grant placed energetic and capable Philip Sheridan, standing at left in this postwar group portrait, in command of the Army of the Shenandoah, with orders to dispose of Early. His able subordinates included *(left to right)* Wesley Merritt, George Crook, James W. Forsyth, and George A. Custer.

Led by skirmishers, Ricketts' 3d division charges up a wooded hill near Berryville Road about noon on September 19, 1864. The Union attack faltered when XIX Corps, on Ricketts' right, failed to advance.

Confederate Gen. Robert E. Rodes, mortally wounded, is helped aboard an ambulance amid his division's retreat from the Federals along the Berryville road.

Union			Confederate	
Inf.	Cav.		Inf.	Cav.
		2 a.m. 9 a.m.		
		11 a.m. 2:30 p.m.		
		4:30 p.m. 5 p.m.		
		5 p.m. 6 p.m.		

With the Army of the Potomac now pressing hard on Lee's defenses around Richmond and Petersburg, Grant was confident that Lee would soon be forced to recall reinforcements he had sent to Early, now back in the Valley after his abortive raid. A week after Grant had instructed Sheridan to be ready to exploit such a development, Early was ordered to give up Kershaw's division, reducing his strength to about 14,000 men. When, on September 17, Early boldly took Gordon's and Rodes' divisions north from Winchester to threaten Maryland, Sheridan seized the opportunity to attack the forces left behind under Ramseur and Wharton. Sheridan proposed a classic double envelopment, using Wright's VI Corps and Emory's XIX Corps to attack and hold from the east, while Sheridan's cavalry swept around from the north and Crook's VIII Corps struck from the south. On September 18, as Sheridan prepared his attack, Early, 20 miles away at Martinsburg, learned of Grant's recent visit to Sheridan; he took the two

divisions with him on a forced march back to Winchester. Sheridan's predawn attack on the 19th met with some success but was hampered by the Federal troops in the rear. Early thus gained time to reunite his command around Winchester, but Sheridan, with more than 30,000 men, still outnumbered him. By 11:00 a.m., after nearly eight hours of seesaw fighting, the Confederate divisions of Breckinridge, Rodes, Gordon, and Ramseur had been forced back into an L-shaped defensive line north and east of Winchester. Their lines held until midafternoon, when a prolonged lull made Early believe he had won "a splendid victory." But at about 4:30 p.m., all three Federal corps, supported by the cavalry divisions of Merritt and Averell, attacked along the entire line. A half-hour later, Merritt's charge broke through Early's left flank, precipitating a Confederate rout. Winchester had changed hands for the 73d and last time, and Early's forces fled in disarray, having suffered 4,000 casualties to Sheridan's 5,000.

CEDAR CREEK

Confederates of Joseph Kershaw's division overrun a Federal camp at Cedar Creek in a surprise dawn attack on October 19. Stripped of anything that might rattle or clink, the attackers had crept into position in the darkness. Many Union soldiers fled before them without their guns, hats, or shoes. A few Union units managed to form battle lines, but most were, as one Federal officer put it, "stolidly, doggedly determined to go to the rear."

Maj. Gen. Stephen D. Ramseur, one of Early's youngest and ablest division commanders, hoped a victory at Cedar Creek would enable him to take leave to visit his wife and new baby daughter. Instead, he was mortally wounded while trying to rally his men during Sheridan's counterattack in the afternoon.

ORDER OF BATTLE

ARMY OF THE VALLEY
EARLY
21,000 MEN

WHARTON'S DIVISION
READ'S BRIGADE
LOGAN'S BRIGADE
SMITH'S BRIGADE

KERSHAW'S DIVISION
GOGGIN'S BRIGADE
HUMPHREYS' BRIGADE
WOFFORD'S BRIGADE
SIMMS' BRIGADE

"SECOND CORPS"
GORDON

PEGRAM'S DIVISION
HOFFMAN'S BRIGADE
JOHNSTON'S BRIGADE
DAVIS' BRIGADE

RAMSEUR'S DIVISION
GRIMES' BRIGADE
COX'S BRIGADE
COOK'S BRIGADE
BATTLE'S BRIGADE

GORDON'S DIVISION (EVANS)
LOWE'S BRIGADE
TERRY'S BRIGADE
PENDLETON'S BRIGADE

CAVALRY

LOMAX'S DIVISION
McCAUSLAND'S BRIGADE
JOHNSON'S BRIGADE
JACKSON'S BRIGADE
IMBODEN'S BRIGADE

ROSSER'S DIVISION
FUNSTEN'S BRIGADE
WICKHAM'S BRIGADE
PAYNE'S BRIGADE

ARMY OF THE SHENANDOAH
SHERIDAN/WRIGHT
31,000 MEN

VI CORPS WRIGHT/RICKETTS

FIRST DIVISION: WHEATON
Brigades: PENROSE, HAMBLIN, EDWARDS

SECOND DIVISION: GETTY
Brigades: WARNER, GRANT, BIDWELL

THIRD DIVISION: KEIFER
Brigades: EMERSON, BALL

VIII CORPS CROOK
(ARMY OF WEST VIRGINIA)

FIRST DIVISION: THOBURN
Brigades: WILDES, CURTIS, HARRIS

SECOND DIVISION: HAYES
Brigades: DEVOL, COATES

PROVISIONAL DIVISION: KITCHING

XIX CORPS EMORY

FIRST DIVISION: McMILLAN
Brigades: DAVIS, THOMAS, CURRIE

SECOND DIVISION: GROVER
Brigades: BIRGE, MOLINEUX, MACAULEY, SHUNK

CAVALRY CORPS TORBERT

FIRST DIVISION: MERRITT
Brigades: KIDD, DEVIN, LOWELL (RESERVE)

SECOND DIVISION: POWELL
Brigades: MOORE, CAPEHART

THIRD DIVISION: CUSTER
Brigades: PENNINGTON, WELLS

CONFEDERATE ATTACK

Sheridan pursued Early up the Valley, defeating him again at Fishers Hill on September 22. Then, believing his enemy had fled east across the Blue Ridge, the Federal commander gave up the chase and kept his troops busy laying waste to the Upper Valley between Strasburg and Staunton. Early's army, however, demoralized but still full of fight, had only fallen back to Port Republic and then to Waynesboro. Lee, meanwhile, returned Kershaw's division, plus an artillery battalion and a cavalry brigade, to Early's main force. On October 1, the Confederates, now more than 20,000 strong and enraged by Sheridan's wanton destruction, slipped back into the Valley. After nearly three weeks of probing and heavy skirmishing, Early decided to strike the still-unsuspecting Federals encamped along Cedar Creek, just north of Strasburg. At first light on October 19, the Rebels crossed Cedar Creek and stormed the Federal tent lines, catching the Union troops entirely by surprise. Gordon's three Confederate divisions swept through the camps of Crook's VIII Corps, and Kershaw's division routed Thoburn's two brigades that had been posted about a mile south of the main Federal encampment. The Confederates, pressing their advantage, drove the XIX Corps from an entrenched position near Belle Grove plantation; but between 7:00 and 9:00 a.m., they were slowed by the dogged resistance of the Federal VI Corps. Sheridan, absent when the battle began, arrived at 10:30 a.m. and began rallying his scattered troops on a line north of Middletown.

FEDERAL COUNTERATTACK

By midday, the battle had reached a critical juncture. The Federals had been dealt a heavy blow, but the bulk of the army had taken up solid defensive positions about a mile north of Middletown. The expended Confederates were now attacking piecemeal and were easily repulsed. Concerned about the condition of his command and the Federal cavalry massed beyond his right flank, Early ordered a fateful pause to rest his exhausted men, many of whom had already stopped fighting to plunder food and clothing from the Federal camps. While the Rebels waited, Sheridan formed the largely intact VI and XIX Corps, along with his cavalry, and shortly after 4:00 p.m., he attacked. At first, the Confederates blocked the advance. But when the Federals flanked Gordon's division on the Confederate left, Early's line began to crumble and soon was in retreat, despite a heroic stand by Ramseur's division in the center. Fierce pursuit by Federal cavalry under Custer and Merritt turned the retreat into a rout that continued until the Confederates halted four miles south of Cedar Creek. By nightfall, Early's shattered army had fallen back to New Market. Sheridan's victory was complete. The Army of the Valley was finished as a fighting force, and despite having suffered around 3,000 casualties to the Federal 5,665, it was still outnumbered two to one. The devastated Valley was Confederate no more.

Waving his hat, Philip Sheridan urges men of Crook's shattered VIII Corps forward, shouting, "Follow me! We'll sleep in the old camp tonight!" Artist-correspondent James E. Taylor, who witnessed this scene and later drew it, added, "The responsive shout from the enthusiastic Blue Coats was like a thunder peal, for there was no resisting the magnetism of the man."

Invigorated by Sheridan's arrival on the battlefield, Gen. Lewis Grant's Vermont brigade forms for a counterattack at Cedar Creek as Confederate prisoners *(left foreground)* are hustled away. The Vermonters had given ground grudgingly during the morning action. During the counterattack, they helped break the back of Stephen Ramseur's division.

Horsemen of George Custer's 3d Cavalry Division run down retreating Confederate foot soldiers on Hupp's Hill.

PETERSBURG TO APPOMATTOX

"This is likely to prove a very tedious job," Ulysses S. Grant wrote to his wife, Julia, on June 6, 1864, "but I feel very confident of ultimate success." In spite of the recent bloodbath at Cold Harbor, Grant was optimistic about his new strategy for a Federal victory. After a spring of relentless flanking maneuvers in the Wilderness, the Union commander determined to seize the initiative, pin Lee down, and sever the supply lines that fed his army. On June 12, Grant began to move the Army of the Potomac—and the venue of battle—across the Chickahominy River and south of the James to seize the key rail center of Petersburg. Through this city passed Lee's lifelines: four railroads that linked the Confederate capital of Richmond with the Deep South.

Grant's flanking march to Petersburg was nearly flawless, but it ended in frustration. General William Smith, commander of the XVIII Corps, grew cautious about attacking Petersburg, giving away valuable time to his adversary, General P. G. T. Beauregard. On the night of June 15, with only 2,200 soldiers, Beauregard mounted a valiant defense of Petersburg against an onslaught of 14,000. Although the Confederates lost a portion of the city's defenses, they were able to withdraw and improvise a new line. Thus began the Siege of Petersburg, which would last until the closing days of the War.

By the spring of 1865, after almost nine months of siege, attrition had taken its toll on the weary Confederate forces. The Union war machine was well supplied from its prodigious depot of matériel housed up the James River at City Point, Virginia, while the Confederates—ill-fed, exhausted, and hopelessly outnumbered—lost men they could not replace. As one Southern general remarked, "However bold we might be, however desperately we

**GEN. PIERRE GUSTAVE TOUTANT
BEAUREGARD**

might fight, we were sure in the end to be worn out. It was only a question of a few months, more or less."

When Lee was finally forced from his trenches at Petersburg on April 2, 1865, he led the remnant of his army westward on a desperate quest for food. Lee entertained hopes of marching southwestward to hook up with General Joseph Johnston in the hills of North Carolina, but he could never break contact with the Federals who were in constant pursuit. Although loath to admit it, Lee knew that the end was nigh. The North had almost a million men bearing arms; the south had fewer than 100,000. "There is nothing left for me to do," he told his aides, "but to go and see General Grant and I had rather die a thousand deaths." The two generals signed the surrender document at Appomattox Courthouse on the afternoon of April 9, 1864, and the proud Army of Northern Virginia laid down its arms.

An oil painting by Edward Henry, a Union recruit, depicts the Federals' supply base at City Point, Virginia. As Grant's line of operations moved south, the Union army transformed this quiet hamlet at the confluence of the James and Appomattox rivers into a bustling seaport and railhead.

As early as June 9, Beauregard predicted that Grant would cross the James and advance on Petersburg. Lee disagreed, insisting that the Federal army could never cross the river undetected and that Richmond was the more likely target. Lee was wrong on both counts. Federal boats began taking Winfield Scott Hancock's II Corps across the James on June 14. That same day, engineers under Capt. George Mendell finished erecting a half-mile-long bridge at Wilcox's Landing, and at midnight, Ambrose Burnside's IX Corps led the way across the span, followed by Gouverneur K. Warren's V Corps. James Wilson's cavalry division crossed on June 16, followed by Horatio G. Wright's VI Corps, which had stayed on the north side of the James to cover the crossing. By the 17th, all of the army except some wagons and guards were on the south side. The plan, though complicated and dangerous, was flawlessly executed.

Men of the 22d U.S. Colored Troops capture a Confederate entrenchment on the Dimmock Line outside Petersburg on June 16, 1864. During the siege of Petersburg and Richmond, 38 black regiments served with the Union armies, more than in any other campaign of the Civil War.

A regiment of Smith's XVIII Corps overruns a portion of the Confederate defenses at Petersburg on the night of June 15. Woefully short of troops, Beauregard had to space his infantrymen at intervals of 10 feet along the eastern four miles of the line.

On June 14, as the Federals crossed the James River, Beauregard had only Henry Wise's Virginia Brigade and the local militia, a total of about 2,200 men, to defend Petersburg. The Confederate commander did possess extensive fortifications. Called the Dimmock Line for the engineer who designed it, this chain of redans—triangular projections open in the rear and designed to allow for both frontal and flanking fire—was connected by almost 10 miles of entrenchments. Ditches and felled trees, or abatis, fronted the redans to obstruct any hostile advance. But the strength of the line depended on sufficient forces to man it, something Beauregard sorely lacked. William Farrah "Baldy" Smith's XVIII Corps, supported by August Kautz's cavalry, attacked Petersburg at 7:00 p.m. on June 15 with a force some 14,000 strong and quickly rolled over a mile-long section of Beauregard's works, from redans 3 through 11. Meanwhile, additional reinforcements had arrived in the form of Hancock's II Corps. The road to Petersburg was wide open—yet Smith stopped short. Trying to explain one of the War's gravest errors of generalship, he reported the next day, "Deeming that I held important points of the enemy's line of works, I thought it prudent to make no further advance." Smith's poor performance stood in contrast to that of his opponent, General Beauregard. Fiery and flamboyant, he served the Confederacy brilliantly that night by feverishly building a new line of defenses that would hold off the Union siege for almost 10 months.

Troops of Burnside's IX Corps, supported by artillery, charge the Confederate defenses at the crater shortly after the July 30 explosion *(above)*. Eight hours later, Gen. William Mahone's men drove the Federals back in bitter hand-to-hand combat *(left)*. The Union lost some 4,400 men at the Crater in what Grant called "the saddest affair I have ever witnessed in the War." He labeled the attack a "stupendous failure—and all due to inefficiency on the part of the corps commander and the incompetency of the division commander who was sent to lead the assault."

In July 1864, frustrated by efforts to take Petersburg, General Meade accepted Lt. Col. Henry Pleasants' scheme to breach the defenses. Pleasants' 48th Pennsylvania, made up mostly of coal miners from Schuylkill County, dug a 511-foot tunnel to a salient in the Confederate line, where a cross shaft was dug and loaded with four tons of gunpowder. The mine was blown early on July 30, and the way was opened for the attack. Spearheaded by Gen. James Ledlie's division, four divisions in Burnside's corps were to pour through the gap and assault the Rebels. But the blast stunned the soldiers, and they became confused in the debris-filled trenches that surrounded the 30-foot-deep, 70-foot-wide crater. Many rushed into the fissure rather than around it. The rear lip of the crater, backed by a Confederate earthwork, proved insurmountable. At a time when the Federals most needed leadership, General Ledlie huddled with a jug of rum in a rear bombproof. The widespread confusion gave the Confederates time to recover from the assault and shore up their defenses. By 9:00 a.m., when Edward Ferrero's black division joined the battle, the Rebels were fending off attacks on both sides of the crater. Confederate Gen. William Mahone began a counterattack about 1:00 p.m. David Weisiger's Virginia Brigade met the front line of Ferrero's troops west of the crater and repulsed them, dashing hopes for a Union breakthrough.

Scale in Feet

0   250   500   1,000

By summer 1864, the fighting around Petersburg had settled into a pattern. Assaults north of the James, at Deep Bottom, and south of the river, at the Weldon Railroad, Reams' Station, and Poplar Springs Church, had tightened the Federals' noose. Yet when the chance for a breakthrough came at the end of September, the Yankees faltered. The Rebels held a fortified camp north of the James at Chaffin's Bluff, eight miles from Richmond. Grant planned to threaten the Confederate capital and tie down en-emy troops that might be needed to reinforce Jubal Early, who was raising havoc in the Shenandoah Valley. Grant ordered Maj. Gen. Ord's XVIII Corps (Ord had replaced Smith) to assail Fort Harrison, on the camp's southeast corner. On the morning of September 29, the Federals swiftly overwhelmed the garrison and its 800 inexperienced artillerists. The way to Richmond was nearly open—but Ord's men fell into disorder and Confederate reinforcements arrived to stall the Federal drive.

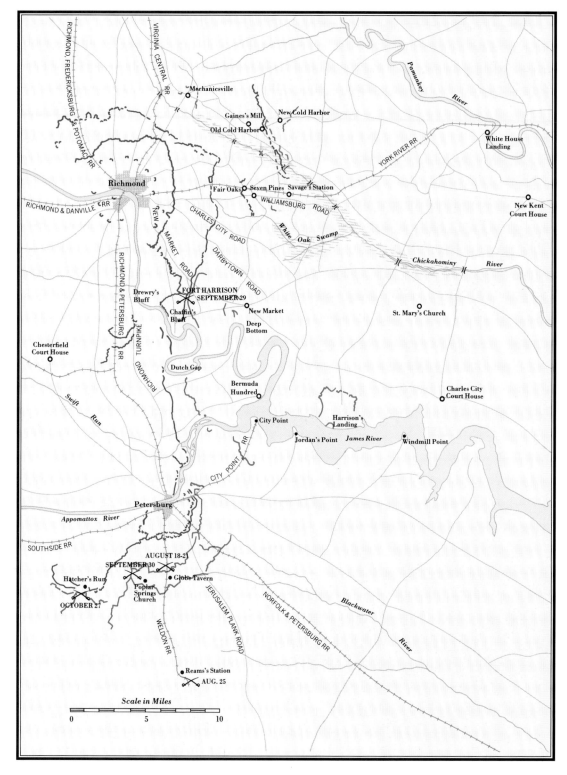

The Federals attacking Fort Harrison faced a daunting obstacle: a parapet with enclosed gun positions, fronted by a fraise—a row of sharpened stakes to frustrate charging infantry.

MAJ. GEN. EDWARD ORD

After destroying track along the Weldon Railroad, Hancock's II Corps *(foreground)* came under assault at Reams' Station by A. P. Hill on August 25. Hill's Confederates pushed the Federals back.

Three hundred Confederates, a select force from Maj. Gen. John Gordon's 2d Corps, pour through openings cut by axmen in the abatis shielding Fort Stedman, a redoubt in the Federal line besieging Petersburg.

The 3d Division of Parke's IX Corps (previously Burnside's), led by Brig. Gen. John F. Hartranft, launches the charge that recaptured Fort Stedman on March 25. The Confederates, Hartranft said, "were forced back into the works in such masses that the victors were scarcely able to deploy among the crowds of prisoners."

Federal gun positions reinforced by gabions—earth-filled baskets—remain standing after the Battle of Fort Stedman. It was nearly impossible for the Confederates to maintain formation within the earthworks, connecting trenches, and dugouts.

Union success on all fronts forced Lee to stage a desperate attack on Fort Stedman, a Union strongpoint east of Petersburg. Striking before dawn on March 25, Gen. John Gordon's men captured the fort and adjoining batteries: nos. 10, 11, and 12. The Confederates then moved beyond Stedman to seize smaller works and widen the gap in the enemy line.

At 7:30 a.m., however, John Hartranft's 3d Division led a spirited countercharge that forced Gordon back into Fort Stedman. When Lee sent orders to withdraw at 8:00, many Confederates chose to surrender because their line of retreat was threatened by cross fire. The Union had turned aside Lee's last, great effort to break its grip on Petersburg.

In what was the final major battle of the Petersburg campaign, Grant sent Philip Sheridan's cavalry, along with some infantry units, to envelop the Confederate right flank southwest of Petersburg. Grant hoped not only to cut the Southside Railroad, a vital Confederate supply line, but to block Lee's escape to the west. Lee dispatched George Pickett's division and W. H. F. Lee's cavalry corps to counter the Federals. By 1:00 p.m. on April 1, Sheridan had deployed Wesley Merritt's cavalry division to expel Pickett's Confederates from their entrenched position at Five Forks. Sheridan planned to pin down Pickett with the cavalry while Gouverneur Warren's V Corps assaulted the Confederate left. It was 4:00 p.m. before Warren came into action, and because of faulty deployment, V Corps nearly missed its objective, striking 800 yards too far to the east. Although Sheridan had agonized over the delay, it proved beneficial. Lulled by the failure of the Federals to attack, Pickett and W. H. F. Lee had left the field just after 2:00 p.m. to enjoy a shad bake on the north bank of Hatcher's Run. Meanwhile, Warren redirected his attack and struck Pickett on his left flank and rear, just as Merritt hit Pickett's front and Mackenzie circled his left. By 7:00 p.m., the Rebels had been decimated in what a Confederate commander later called the "Waterloo of the Confederacy."

Lee chose his nephew, Maj. Gen. Fitzhugh Lee, to lead the cavalry forces countering Sheridan's attack at Five Forks.

Ranald Mackenzie commanded the cavalry division of the Army of the James during the battle.

Two brigades of Gen. George Armstrong Custer's 3d Cavalry Division charge a line of Virginians on the Confederate far right at Five Forks. Because of the difficult terrain, the remainder of Custer's brigades fought on foot.

ROBERTS

MACKENZIE

Boisseau House

Chimneys

Sydnor House

CRAWFORD

MAYO

PICKETT

WALLACE

RANSOM

Angle

Five Forks

STUART

PEGRAM

MAYO

WHITE OAK ROAD

CORSE

W.H.F. LEE

CAPEHART

WELLS

Gilliam House

PENNINGTON

FITZHUGH

STAGG

GIBBS

DEVIN

Gravelly Run Church

CRAWFORD

GRIFFIN

AYRES

WARREN
V CORPS

CRUMP ROAD

CUSTER

MERRITT

Jas. Boisseau
House

SCOTT'S ROAD

DINWIDDIE

ROAD

RUN

COURT

HOUSE

ROAD

GRAVELLY

Scott House

Bear Swamp

GREGG

J. Boisseau House

CRAWFORD

GRIFFIN

BROCK'S

AYRES
ROAD

FORD'S DEPOT ROAD

Chamberlain's

Creek

MACKENZIE

to Dinwiddie Court House

Scale in Miles

0   ½   1   2

Galvanized by word of Sheridan's success at Five Forks, Grant's forces at Petersburg launched a concentrated assault on the weakened Confederate defenses at dawn on April 2. On the Union right, Maj. Gen. John Parke's IX Corps captured—but failed to hold—Fort Mahone, known to the Federals as Fort Damnation. Elsewhere, however, Maj. Gen. Horatio Wright's VI Corps broke through A. P. Hill's lines west of Petersburg, cutting Boydton Plank Road and the Southside Railroad. Hill was killed in the assault. On hearing of his trusted commander's death, a desolate Lee murmured, "He is at rest now and we who are left are the ones to suffer." In desperation, Lee withdrew to the innermost line of defense. By nightfall, Maj. John Gibbon's XXIV Corps had taken Fort Gregg and forced the evacuation of Fort Mahone. Lee had no choice but to evacuate Petersburg.

Standing atop a breastwork at Petersburg, a lone Confederate invites enemy fire in this 1864 painting by Winslow Homer. Although Homer used his imagination here, such acts were not uncommon. One man in the trenches pondered whether those who took such risks were seeking a swift end to their ordeal: "It was enough to make men mad and reckless."

LT. GEN. AMBROSE POWELL HILL

Pushing aside chevaux-de-frise, the 2d Division of Parke's IX Corps storms Fort Mahone during the climactic Federal attack on the works around Petersburg *(bottom)*. The following morning, a Confederate soldier lies dead among the scattered detritus of war.

BRIG. GEN. DON CARLOS BUELL

FEDERAL COUNTERATTACK, APRIL 7

Believing that victory was his and that Grant was about to flee across the Tennessee, Beauregard made no attempt during the night of April 6-7 to form a defense or to replenish his ammunition. But Grant was shuffling Buell's brigades into his line and preparing to counterattack. At dawn on the seventh, Federal skirmishers moved forward, followed by the bulk of both Union armies, about 45,000 men versus only 20,000 Confederates still able to fight. As the Union attack ground ahead, several Confederate units made desperate charges into the Federal front. Taking the initiative when Federal progress slowed, Patrick Cleburne's brigade of Hardee's corps smashed into the Union center near the road to Corinth—and lost 1,700 men killed or wounded. Benjamin Cheatham's brigade reinforced Cleburne to attack Gen. Thomas Crittenden's division in the Federal center. Around Shiloh Church, remnants of Gen. Dan Ruggles' division and Gen. Sterling A. M. Wood's brigade put up savage resistance. But as more Federal brigades came into action, the Confederates were pushed back. Shortly after 2:30, Beauregard ordered a withdrawal, forming a rear guard and sending the rest of his army trudging toward Corinth, burning the captured Federal camps as they withdrew. The Federals, also spent, and bogged down by heavy rains, did not pursue. The casualties for the two-day battle were shocking and nearly equal: Each side lost about 1,700 killed and roughly 8,000 wounded. Grant, criticized for the near defeat, was briefly shunted to a meaningless post, and Gen. Henry Halleck, commander in chief in the West, took over the Federal army. Halleck did not push the Confederate army out of Corinth until May 29.

GEN. P. G. T. BEAUREGARD

Beauregard *(second from the right)* reins up with his staff next to Shiloh Church about 2:00 p.m. on April 7. He soon sent aides to the Confederate corps commanders with orders to retreat. At top right are the tents of Sherman's camp, overrun on the battle's first day.

After Shiloh, the war in the West split into two loosely interdependent campaigns. One was the long, arduous Federal attempt, overseen by Ulysses S. Grant, to gain control of the Mississippi River. The other was a sprawling contest for control of middle and eastern Tennessee. It began with an ambitious Confederate invasion of Kentucky—a campaign of marching and countermarching that ranged from the Alabama-Tennessee border northward 350 miles to the Ohio River.

The campaign began when General Don Carlos Buell's Army of the Ohio began a slow advance from Corinth, Mississippi, toward another vital Confederate rail junction at Chattanooga. To divert Buell from this target, General Edmund Kirby Smith, clever and ambitious commander of Confederate forces in East Tennessee, boldly decided to strike north into Kentucky with a small army from his base at Knoxville. After vacillating for several weeks, General Braxton Bragg decided to join in the action, bringing his army from its base at Tupelo, Mississippi, to Chattanooga, and then northward on a parallel track. Bragg, initially reluctant to move, soon embraced the campaign with fervor, believing that thousands of pro-Southern Tennesseans and Kentuckians would flock to join his army and that a successful invasion would not only force Buell's army out of Tennessee but maybe even bring Kentucky into the Confederacy.

Buell was compelled to pursue Bragg and Kirby Smith. His progress was slow; Buell was methodical to a fault and his supply lines were constantly beset by bands of Confederate cavalry. But in September he reached Louisville, then doubled back to meet Bragg. At Perryville, in October, the two forces collided violently. Bragg, realizing he was seriously outnum-

General Braxton Bragg was given command of the Confederate army in northern Mississippi in June 1862, replacing General Beauregard, who had abandoned Corinth without a fight.

bered, broke off the fight and retreated 200 miles to Knoxville. At the end of the month, President Jefferson Davis, concerned about the mounting criticism of Bragg's abilities, summoned the general to Richmond. Davis was satisfied with Bragg's explanation that the retreat had been a military necessity, but the rift between Bragg and his generals would never heal. Back in Tennessee, the army commander prepared his forces for an advance on Nashville, while John Hunt Morgan's Rebel cavalry played havoc with Union supply lines.

At length, the Federals under General William S. Rosecrans, who had replaced the timid Buell, caught up with Bragg again, this time near Murfreesboro, Tennessee, where the Confederate general had gathered his forces in late November and December. There, at year's end, on the banks of Stones River, Bragg attacked with a ferocity that nearly won a decisive victory. But showing a strange loss of nerve and judgment, the general failed to press his advantage and retreated once more. The battle ended as a major victory for the North. Kentucky was safe at last and Nashville made secure as a base for future Federal operations.

Taking the offensive in mid-August 1862, Kirby Smith first sent Gen. Carter Stevenson to pry a Federal force under George Morgan from the Cumberland Gap; then both Stevenson and Kirby Smith, with 20,000 men, marched on to Lexington and Frankfort. Later that month, Bragg, with about 30,000 men, moved north along a parallel route to the west, intending to join Kirby Smith in capturing the vital Union supply center at Louisville. Forced to abandon the drive on Chattanooga, the 55,000-man Federal army under Buell started in pursuit over several routes, reuniting in Kentucky and managing to reach Louisville before the Confederates arrived. Once there, Buell turned his divisions about and collided with part of Bragg's Confederate army at Perryville on October 8. After the inconclusive battle, Bragg, outnumbered and fearful for his supply lines, headed back to Tennessee, eventually concentrating at Murfreesboro. The Federals returned to Nashville where they gathered their strength under their new commander, Gen. William S. Rosecrans. On December 26, they marched out to the southeast looking for a fight with General Bragg.

General William Rufus Terrill, disowned by his Virginia family for remaining faithful to the Union, was killed by a Confederate shell while urging his brigade to hold the Federal left at Perryville.

Major General Benjamin Franklin Cheatham, though distrusted by Bragg as an incompetent political appointee, led his Tennessee infantry in a disciplined attack at Perryville. "Cheatham's noble division," one officer recalled, "moved forward as if on dress parade."

In a cornfield on the Federal left, men of Col. John C. Starkweather's brigade level a volley at George Maney's Confederates advancing through the stalks. Starkweather's grim defense prevented Benjamin Cheatham's division from turning the Federal flank.

A log house stands among meadows on the high ground near the intersection of Benton Road and Mackville Pike, where McCook's Federals were finally able to stem the Confederate advance.

The Battle of Perryville
nearly ended in disaster
for General Bragg, who,
believing that most of
the Federal army was far
to the north, marching
from Louisville toward
Frankfort, sent 16,000
Confederates under Le-
onidas Polk into the
path of Buell's entire
force of some 60,000
men. At 2:00 p.m. on
October 8, Bragg
ordered Cheatham's di-
vision across the Chap-
lin River to attack the
Federal left. Cheatham's
rush broke Jackson's
division, and follow-up
attacks by Buckner's and
part of Anderson's divi-
sions drove back the
rest of McCook's corps.
But in the center, Sheri-
dan repulsed Ander-
son's other two bri-
gades, and by nightfall,
the exhausted Confeder-
ates halted their attacks.
Bragg, at last realizing
that he was vastly out-
numbered, broke off the
battle and retreated,
saved from possible an-
nihilation by the failure
of General Crittenden to
advance his Federal II
Corps and envelop the
Confederate left.

209

GEN. LEONIDAS POLK

GEN. WILLIAM J. HARDEE

ORDER OF BATTLE
ARMY OF TENNESSEE
BRAGG
34,700 MEN

POLK'S CORPS

FIRST DIVISION: CHEATHAM	**SECOND DIVISION: WITHERS**
Brigades: DONELSON, STEWART, MANEY, VAUGHN	*Brigades:* LOOMIS, CHALMERS, ANDERSON, MANIGAULT

HARDEE'S CORPS

FIRST DIVISION: BRECKENRIDGE	**SECOND DIVISION: CLEBURNE**
Brigades: ADAMS, PALMER, PRESTON, HANSON, JACKSON	*Brigades:* L. E. POLK, LIDDELL, JOHNSON, WOOD

McCOWN'S DIVISION
Brigades: ECTOR, RAINS, McNAIR

CAVALRY
WHEELER

WHEELER'S BRIGADE	PEGRAM'S BRIGADE
BUFORD'S BRIGADE	WHARTON'S BRIGADE

ARMY OF THE CUMBERLAND
ROSECRANS
41,400 MEN

LEFT WING CRITTENDEN	**CENTER THOMAS**	**RIGHT WING McCOOK**
FIRST DIVISION: WOOD	FIRST DIVISION: ROUSSEAU	FIRST DIVISION: DAVIS
Brigades: HASCALL, WAGNER, HARKER	*Brigades:* SCRIBNER, BEATTY, STARKWEATHER, SHEPHARD	*Brigades:* POST, CARLIN, WOODRUFF
SECOND DIVISION: PALMER	SECOND DIVISION: NEGLEY	SECOND DIVISION: JOHNSON
Brigades: CRUFT, HAZEN, GROSE	*Brigades:* SPEARS, STANLEY, MILLER	*Brigades:* WILLICH, KIRK, BALDWIN
THIRD DIVISION: VAN CLEVE	THIRD DIVISION: FRY	THIRD DIVISION: SHERIDAN
Brigades: BEATTY, FYFFE, PRICE	WALKER'S BRIGADE ONLY	*Brigades:* SILL, SCHAEFER, ROBERTS
	FOURTH DIVISION (two regiments only)	
	FIFTH DIVISION (not engaged)	

CAVALRY
STANLEY

CAVALRY DIVISION: KENNETT
Brigades: MINTY, ZAHM

OPENING CONFEDERATE ATTACKS, DECEMBER 31, 1862

For two months after the Battle of Perryville, fighting between the armies was limited to heavy skirmishing along Federal supply lines. Gen. William Rosecrans *(right)*, having taken over from the slow-moving Buell, holed up in Nashville reorganizing his new command. Bragg, who had retreated into Tennessee, advanced north in early November to the Murfreesboro's area—and waited for Rosecrans to move. On the day after Christmas, Rosecrans started his advance toward Murfreesboro; by December 30, the two armies were drawn up for battle along the icy Stones River with each commander planning to attack the other's right flank. Needing a quick victory, Bragg struck first, sending Hardee's 10,000 men on the Confederate left dashing forward at dawn on the 31st in a sustained assault against Mc-

Cook's corps. By 8:00 a.m., Gen. John Mc-Cown's Rebels had shattered Johnson's division on the Union far right. At the same time, Cleburne's division hammered away at Davis' three Federal brigades, who put up a stiff fight until they were outflanked. General Polk's corps also advanced, attacking the Federal center held by Sheridan's, Palmer's, and Negley's divisions, but Polk's assaults failed to break through, and the battered Union troops were able to fall back and form a new line to face the threat to their flank. Meanwhile, on the Federal left, Rosecrans had initiated his own attack, sending Van Cleve's division across Stones River. But before the next units could cross, frantic appeals from McCook and the sound of heavy fighting to the south forced him to call off the attack to deal with the threat to his right.

212

Colonel William P. Hazen, a West Pointer who had commanded the 41st Ohio at Shiloh and Perryville, held the Round Forest with his four-regiment brigade of Palmer's division for most of December 31, forming the pivot of the Federal defense.

In one of a series of remarkably accurate pictures of the battle done by a Union soldier, Pvt. Alfred Mathews, Confederate troops *(background, right)* advance in disciplined lines. They were slaughtered by fire from Federal infantry and artillery, drawn up north of the Round Forest between the Nashville Pike *(right)* and the railroad.

FINAL CONFEDERATE ATTACKS

By midmorning on December 31, the Federal right had been jackknifed almost 90 degrees from its original position by Hardee's continuing assaults. The Federal center had also been driven in by the furious attacks of Cheatham's and Withers' divisions against Sheridan's and Palmer's positions. The Confederate assaults were slowed, however, as General Rosecrans, riding forward to take charge of the Federal defense, funneled reinforcements to the threatened parts of his line. Giving up his original idea of having Crittenden's corps cross Stones River to attack Bragg's right flank, Rosecrans began stripping his left, sending parts of Van Cleve's and Wood's divisions across the rear of the battlefield to help the remnants of McCook's men hold their line. At the same time, Rosecrans moved Rousseau's division into position along Nashville Pike to back up Sheridan and Negley. He also deployed other units to reinforce Palmer and brought up battery after battery of guns to support the infantry. Despite the stiffening resistance, Polk continued to attack, hammering back Sheridan's and Negley's weary troops. This exposed Palmer's division in the nose of the salient formed by the V-shaped Federal line. Particularly vulnerable was the brigade under William Hazen that was holding a grove called the Round Forest. Beginning around 2:00 p.m., Hazen's position was attacked first by two brigades from Polk's corps and finally just before dark by four brigades from Breckinridge's division brought over from the Confederate right. But all the assaults were thrown back, the attackers scythed down by furious fire from Hazen's troops and supporting units, and from the Federal guns lined up virtually hub-to-hub. As night fell, Bragg, his army having suffered dreadful losses, ended the battle for the day.

In another of Private Mathews' pictures, the Ohio, Indiana, and Kentucky troops of Samuel Beatty's brigade *(foreground)*, moving quickly to reinforce the Federal right, stagger Patrick Cleburne's attacking Confederates with a sharp volley about noon on the first day of the battle.

BRECKINRIDGE'S ATTACK, JANUARY 2, 1863

Certain he had scored a crushing victory that would send the Federals fleeing to Nashville, Bragg was shocked to find Rosecrans' army still firmly in place on January 1 and ready to fight. The shock produced a strange lethargy, and for the entire day, Bragg did virtually nothing. Finally, on the afternoon of January 2, he impulsively ordered Breckinridge's division to attack four Union brigades under General Beatty that Rosecrans had sent to occupy a ridge just east of Stones River. At precisely 4:00 p.m., Breckinridge's troops stormed the height and in 45 minutes of furious fighting, drove Beatty's men back across the river. But the advance exposed the Confederates to murderous fire from Maj. John Mendenhall's 58 Federal guns massed on the river's west bank. Shortly, elements of Negley's division, followed by Palmer's, counterattacked across the river and swept Breckinridge back to his starting point. With this dismal failure, Bragg ended the battle. The next day, he began a retreat into southern Tennessee, leaving the field—and most of the state—securely in Union hands.

General James S. Negley, whose Federal division counterattacked across Stones River on January 2, was a stout, affable 36-year-old who had served as a private in the Mexican War. In civilian life, Negley had been a well-known horticulturist.

The 2,200 men of Col.
John Miller's brigade
of Negley's division
ford Stones River to pur-
sue the remnants of
Breckinridge's Confed-
erates. The headlong
Federal counterattack
was halted only by the
early-winter darkness.

A view looking west
across Stones River
shows the hill where
Crittenden's chief of ar-
tillery, Maj. John Men-
denhall, placed his guns
to repel Breckinridge's
assault. When the Feder-
als opened fire, one ob-
server wrote, it must
have seemed to the
Confederate troops that
they had "opened the
door of Hell, and the
devil himself was there
to greet them."

MISSISSIPPI RIVER CAMPAIGN

In the spring of 1862, the Union army and navy together began one of the most difficult as well as important campaigns of the War—the long, arduous effort to seize control of the lower Mississippi River, cut the Confederate supply lines across it, and open the great waterway to Northern commerce moving from the Midwest to New Orleans and the sea.

The first moves went well for the Federals, a fleet under Admiral David Glasgow Farragut rather handily taking New Orleans. But the navy and a Union army under Ulysses S. Grant found the main upriver Confederate stronghold of Vicksburg extraordinarily hard to crack. Bombardments by gunboats achieved nothing.

Equally fruitless were Grant's repeated attempts through the fall and winter of 1862-1863 to take the city from the rear. Finally, in the spring, the determined Grant managed to move down the Mississippi past Vicksburg's guns and land his army on the river's east bank. From there, he pushed northward, battling Confederate forces at Port Gibson, Champion's Hill, and Jackson before at last closing in on Vicksburg itself and beginning a long siege that ultimately forced the city's surrender. With that stunning blow to the Southern cause, the defenders of the other Rebel citadel at Port Hudson also gave up, prompting a satisfied President Lincoln to remark: "The Father of Waters again goes unvexed to the sea."

Having secured most of the lower Mississippi, Farragut sailed his fleet upriver, bombarding Vicksburg in June with no success. Grant, trying to drive on the city from the north, was delayed by two Confederate thrusts *(red lines)* at his supply lines led by Earl Van Dorn and Nathan B. Forrest. But in late 1862, Grant had two Union corps moving down the Mississippi River: John McClernand's taking a Confederate fort at Arkansas Post en route and William T. Sherman's making a first failed attack on Vicksburg's outer defenses at Chickasaw Bluffs. By January 1863, the bulk of Grant's army was at Milliken's Bend, ready to begin the main struggle for Vicksburg.

Dominated by its Greek revival courthouse, which was completed in 1860, Vicksburg looks westward over a wide stretch of the Mississippi. The city, constructed on a series of bluffs, loomed like a fortress over the river; to the north and east it was protected by a maze of bayous and bogs.

Confederate Brig. Gen. Johnson K. Duncan salutes as he boards the Federal gunboat *Harriet Lane* to surrender Forts Jackson and St. Philip to Cdr. David Porter, who waits at the top of the gangway. The fall of the forts on April 28, 1862, left New Orleans defenseless, and the city was occupied the next day.

Farragut's fleet, one of the largest ever assembled in the United States, blasts past Fort Jackson *(foreground)* and Fort St. Philip before dawn on April 24, 1862. Earlier, two Federal gunboats had opened the way by cutting a passage through the massive iron chains *(bottom right)* the Confederates had strung as a barrier across the river. Despite furious fire from the two forts' heavy batteries and attacks by a small Confederate flotilla, Farragut's losses were amazingly light—one ship sunk and 37 men killed. By midday, the Union fleet was steaming upriver unchallenged.

219

To pry open the lower reaches of the Mississippi, David Farragut assembled a fleet at Ship Island off Biloxi and sailed toward the river's delta in March 1862. The smaller ships, including a flotilla of 19 mortar-carrying schooners led by Cdr. David D. Porter, made it through the Pass à l'Outre; Farragut's larger vessels bulled their way through the deeper Southwest Pass. On April 18, Porter's schooners began lobbing shells into Forts Jackson and St. Philip, the Confederate bastions guarding the river. The bombardment did only superficial damage to the formidable stone ramparts, however, and after five days, Farragut, weary of waiting, boldly sailed his heavy sloops of war and gunboats clear past the forts. Both strongholds surrendered when an 18,000-man Union army under Gen. Benjamin F. Butler, landing on the shore of Isle au Breton Sound, threatened to take them from the rear. By April 25, Farragut's fleet had passed New Orleans' last puny defenses and in May took Baton Rouge.

MAJ. GEN. EARL VAN DORN

Attempting to break Grant's hold on northern Mississippi before the Federals could drive on Vicksburg, Confederate Gen. Earl Van Dorn moved north with 10,000 troops and joined a force of 17,000 led by Sterling Price for an attack on the key Union supply depot at Corinth. On October 3, 1862, three of Van Dorn's divisions swiftly pushed back the first Union line. But the town's Federal defenders, led by Gen. William Rosecrans, re-formed and stubbornly held a second line of recently dug earthworks until darkness brought an end to the fighting. The next morning, Van Dorn's Confederates attacked again, his regiments smashing into the center of the Federal entrenchments. Col. William Rogers' Texans broke through only to be slaughtered by volleys from Rosecrans' reserves. By 11:30 a.m., the battle was over and Van Dorn's crippled force was in full flight.

Earl Van Dorn, a 42-year-old West Pointer *(below left)*, rashly sent his Confederate troops in head-on attacks against the Federals' strong inner earthworks at Corinth on October 3 and 4, 1862. The scene at left shows Col. William Rogers, whose 2d Texas spearheaded the disastrous assault, being shot dead while waving the regiment's colors from the parapet of a Union strongpoint called Battery Robinett. In the photograph below, Federal soldiers survey the carnage after the battle, including Rogers' body, which lies just left of the tree stump at center.

David Porter's Federal flotilla braves Confederate fire from batteries along the shore and on the bluffs at Vicksburg during a daring night run on April 16, 1863. Barges and transports, lashed to the gunboats for protection, carried men and supplies to landing sites downriver for Grant's assault on Vicksburg from the south.

Federal troops engage in the grueling task of dredging a canal across a bend in the Mississippi opposite Vicksburg that would have given Porter's ships a detour past the fortress' guns. Grant had little faith that this and other amphibious schemes would work but thought them worth a try. They also kept the soldiers busy during the rainy, muddy winter when offensive operations on land were impossible. "I let the work go on," he wrote, "believing employment was better than idleness."

FLANKING ATTEMPTS, DECEMBER 1862-MARCH 1863

On the west bank of the Mississippi, Grant began building a canal across from Vicksburg. Farther north, James McPherson cut a passage to Lake Providence, ships could navigate the bayous south to the Red River. On the east bank, 325 miles above the city, Union engineers breached a levee at Yazoo Pass, letting Mississippi water flood the Yazoo, making it navigable. The scheme was foiled when Gen. W. W. Loring's Confederates built Fort Pemberton at a bend in the river. To support the expedition, Sherman and his naval ally David Porter tried pushing up the lower Yazoo into Steele's Bayou, but low water nearly bottled up Porter's fleet. The Union's plans failed, forcing Porter and Grant to run their boats at night past Vicksburg.

MAJ. GEN. ULYSSES S. GRANT

REAR ADM. DAVID DIXON PORTER

MARCH ON VICKSBURG, APRIL-MAY

As Porter's ships landed some of Grant's troops south of Vicksburg at New Carthage, others marched down muddy roads on the Mississippi's west bank. Then, while Sherman distracted Gen. John C. Pemberton, commander of Vicksburg's defenses, with a feint at Haines' Bluff, Grant sent both McClernand's and McPherson's corps across the river to the east bank. There on May 1 they beat back a small but stubborn Confederate force led by Brig. Gen. John S. Bowen at Port Gibson. With Sherman's corps now across the river as well, Grant marched swiftly to get between Pemberton's forces near Vicksburg and strong Rebel reinforcements gathering at Jackson. Near Raymond, McPherson's corps overcame Gen. John Gregg's troops. With McPherson's and Sherman's troops, Grant defeated Joseph E. Johnston at Jackson, taking the town on May 14. Grant then turned west, overcoming Pemberton's three divisions in a fierce battle at Champion's Hill. By May 18, the Federals were in the outskirts of Vicksburg.

MAJ. GEN. JOHN S. BOWEN

MAJ. GEN. JOHN McCLERNAND

CHAMPION'S HILL, MAY 16

Trying to cut Grant's communications and strike his rear, Pemberton sent three divisions westward to intercept the Federals at Champion's Hill. Gen. Alvin Hovey's Union brigade seized the hill on May 16 but was soon flung back in furious fighting by John Bowen's Confederates. Bowen was shortly in trouble, however, as William Loring failed to advance in support. Federal brigades under John Logan and Marcellus Crocker smashed into Carter L. Stevenson's division on the Confederate left flank, and McClernand belatedly ordered Osterhaus' brigade forward to assail the Rebel right. By late afternoon, Pemberton's bloodied troops were in retreat toward Baker's Creek and the roads to Vicksburg.

Braving rounds of double-shotted canister, Indiana troops of Gen. George McGinnis' brigade overwhelm a Confederate battery on the crest of Champion's Hill. In spite of a subsequent Rebel counterattack, Pemberton's army was eventually routed at a cost of 3,839 casualties.

General John C. Pemberton confirmed his reputation as a cautious commander by concentrating his army for a static defense of Vicksburg, rather than boldly driving eastward to link up with another Confederate force under Joseph Johnston and fighting Grant in open battle.

VICKSBURG BESIEGED, MAY-JULY

Having pushed the Rebels back to Vicksburg's defenses, Grant ordered an assault on May 19 that met a violent reception. McPherson and McClernand could not advance through ravines choked with felled trees. Only Sherman on the north made progress, Col. Giles A. Smith storming the Stockade Redans. But Smith was pinned down and escaped only after dark. On May 22, Grant tried again. Some of McClernand's troops, including Lawler's and Landrum's men, reached the top of the Railroad Redoubt only to be beaten back. Grant settled for a siege. On June 25, the Federals tried again, detonating a mine beneath the Jackson Road defenses. McPherson's troops charged through the resulting crater, but made little headway. Vicksburg was taken only after 48 days of shelling and near starvation convinced Pemberton that resistance was futile.

Staggered by a hail of Minié balls and grapeshot, troops of the 22d Iowa struggle up the steep ramparts of the Confederate Railroad Redoubt on May 22, their color sergeant bravely leading the way. All the day's Union attacks were driven back with heavy losses totaling 3,199 men.

XV CORPS
SHERMAN

EWING

Mint Spring Bayou

BALDWIN
VAUGHN
SHOUP
STOCKADE REDAN
COCKRELL

G. A. SMITH

T. K. SMITH

RANSOM

FORT HILL
M. L. SMITH

HEBERT

YAZOO CITY ROAD

Glass Bayou

GRAVEYARD ROAD

JACKSON ROAD

BOWEN

FORNEY

GREEN

MOORE

3RD LA. REDAN

GREAT REDOUBT

J. E. SMITH

XVII CORPS
MCPHERSON

STEVENSON

VICKSBURG

SUPPLY DEPOTS

BALDWIN'S FERRY ROAD

Engine House

2ND TEXAS LUNETTE

RAILROAD REDOUBT

BURBRIDGE

BENTON

LAWLER

XIII CORPS
MCCLERNAND

Two Mile Bridge

De Soto

M I S S I S S I P P I   R I V E R

S. D. LEE

LANDRAM

SOUTHERN MISSISSIPPI RAILROAD

STEVENSON

WARRENTON ROAD

SQUARE FORT

CUMMING

REYNOLDS

Stout's Bayou

SALIENT WORK

BARTON

HALL'S FERRY ROAD

SOUTH FORT

ASSAULT OF MAY 19

ASSAULT OF MAY 22

0   1/4   1/2   1   2

Scale in Miles

In the painting at left, soldiers of the 45th Illinois charge through a trench into the crater made by the explosion of 2,200 pounds of gunpowder under a Confederate redoubt near the Jackson Road. The blast blew away much of the redoubt but killed few defenders. Most of them, anticipating the explosion, had pulled back to a new line—from which they mowed down the Federals with cannon and musket fire before counterattacking. The photograph, taken after the siege, shows the same sections of Union trench and the crater *(upper right)* as well as a curious structure made of railroad ties that was built and used by a celebrated sharpshooter of the 23d Indiana named Henry C. Foster. Because Foster favored a coonskin cap, his perch was dubbed Coonskin Tower.

Accepting the Confederate surrender on July 4, 1863, Grant and his staff approach the Vicksburg house used by Pemberton as his headquarters. Grant's terms were generous—he paroled the entire Confederate garrison instead of making the men prisoners—and he rushed in food to relieve the half-starved city. Despite the bombardments, fewer than a dozen civilians were known to have been killed and about three times that number injured. The news of Vicksburg's surrender caused shock in the South, especially since it came on the same day that Robert E. Lee retreated after the defeat at Gettysburg.

WEITZEL

GROVER

May 27

★
Banks'
Headquarters

SHELBY

STEEDMAN

PAINE

LYLES

June 14

BANKS

GARDNER

BEAL

★
Gardner's
Headquarters

ADGER

MISSISSIPPI RIVER

MILES

June 14

DWIGHT

0   1/2   1
Scale in Miles

Like Vicksburg 120 miles to the north, Port Hudson was situated on high bluffs overlooking a sharp bend in the Mississippi and was protected inland by bayous, thickets, and gullies. The Confederates, 16,000 strong, under Maj. Gen. Franklin Gardner, fortified the town with 19 heavy guns commanding the river and the same number of lighter artillery pieces on the landward side. In the spring of 1863, Gen. Nathaniel P. Banks besieged Port Hudson with 24,000 men and then, becoming impatient, attacked head-on. On May 27, troops from the divisions of Weitzel and Grover advanced, but soon became entangled in dense thickets and mazes of fallen trees and were easily repulsed by the Confederates of Col. I. G. W. Steedman. A two-pronged attack on June 14, by troops under Paine and Dwight, was also a catastrophe for the Federals. Banks' total losses in the two assaults came to nearly 4,000 men. But the Confederates were also in trouble as sickness spread and supplies ran desperately low. When word came that Vicksburg had fallen, Gardner gave up hope and surrendered on July 9.

Federal infantrymen clamber over fallen timbers during one of Banks' attacks on the Port Hudson defenses. Thrown back with heavy losses, the Union troops cursed the entire operation, one officer fuming that "the affair was a gigantic bushwhack." In the two failed attacks, the Federals lost 4,000 dead and wounded. By mid-June, another 7,000 men had fallen ill, many suffering dysentery or sunstroke in the stifling heat of Port Hudson's swamps. By that time, General Gardner's garrison had been reduced to 6,000 men, units having been sent north to help defend Vicksburg.

After the siege, a section of the defensive line called Fort Desperate by the Confederates is a shambles of broken timbers and wrecked cannon. Gardner's men survived bombardment by heavy 20-pounder Parrott rifles by burrowing dugouts in the earth that protected against all but a direct hit. When the surrender finally came, the men from both sides crawled from their trenches and redoubts to shake hands. Port Hudson was especially valuable to the South because its guns blocked Federal river traffic and also guarded the nearby mouth of the Red River, an avenue for goods flowing from the West that helped sustain the Confederacy.

CHATTANOOGA CAMPAIGN

Following the Battle of Stones River, the armies of Braxton Bragg and William Rosecrans sat 30 miles apart in central Tennessee for six months, idle except for cavalry raids on each other's supply lines. Bragg, who had been defeated at Perryville and Stones River, was now the most maligned general in the Confederacy. The soldiers of his Army of Tennessee resented his severe discipline, his officers questioned his competence, and the public despised him for his retreats. It was said that Bragg retreated whether he won or lost; a Confederate joke had it that he would never get to heaven because the moment he was invited to enter he would fall back.

As winter changed to spring, Rosecrans, too, drew criticism—for his failure to take his Army of the Cumberland on the offensive. Despite goading from the Union high command, it was not until June that Rosecrans bestirred himself. When he did, to the surprise of many, Rosecrans acted with boldness and confidence. Maneuvering skillfully, he threatened to outflank Bragg and forced the Confederates to retreat again, this time to Chattanooga.

Geography and the Southern rail system dictated that Chattanooga, an otherwise unremarkable settlement of 3,500 people, play a key role in the War. But when Federal troops closed around this transportation hub on September 6, 1863, the Confederates evacuated it without a fight. Again Bragg was outmaneuvered and had to move his army south or risk being cut off.

Convinced that the Confederates were fleeing, Rosecrans swiftly pursued them into Georgia. But rather than retreat, Bragg stood and fought at Chickamauga Creek, inflicting a stunning blow and sending the Federals reeling. Bragg declined to pursue the Union army. His men were exhausted and both sides had suffered heavy casualties—the Rebels lost 18,454 and the Yankees 16,179 in the bloodiest two days of the War. When Rosecrans' forces withdrew into Chattanooga, Bragg bottled them up and severed their supply lines, imposing a state of siege.

Now it was Rosecrans' turn to be discredited. Remarking that the general was "stunned and confused, like a duck hit on the head," Lincoln relieved him of command and placed the perilous situation in the hands of the North's most trusted leader, Ulysses S. Grant. Losing no time, Grant launched assaults that cleared the Confederates from their positions on the heights of Lookout Mountain and Missionary Ridge. The South would never recover from the loss of Chattanooga, which brought Bragg's dismissal and opened the gateway to the Confederate heartland.

In January 1863, after the repulse at Murfreesboro, Braxton Bragg withdrew to positions around Tullahoma. Pursuing in mid-June with a series of bold flanking moves, William S. Rosecrans forced Bragg to retreat across the Tennessee River to Chattanooga. Rosecrans, after several weeks of delay, advanced to the river, and by early September, most of his army was across the river below Chattanooga and pushing east in three columns. Bragg evacuated the town on September 7, fell back south, and then turned to fight. After botching several attempts to smash Thomas and Crittenden as they emerged from the mountains (inset), the Confederates girded for battle along Chickamauga Creek.

OPENING ACTION, SEPTEMBER 19

By September 13, Rosecrans realized that his three scattered corps were in grave danger. Bragg was clearly massing for a fight, and alarming rumors, soon proved true, were circulating that the Confederates were being reinforced. The Federal commander ordered McCook and Thomas to close up with Crittenden, who had reached Lee and Gordon's Mill after passing through Chattanooga. Bragg, after having missed numerous opportunities to attack, decided to strike Crittenden's left and cut off the three Union corps from Chattanooga. He ordered Bushrod Johnson, Hood (newly arrived from Virginia), Walker, and Buckner to cross to the west bank of the Chickamauga, a stream whose Cherokee name meant River of Blood. The advance got under way on the afternoon of September 18, but skirmishes with Union cavalry and rough mountain roads made the Confederates' progress slow. The fighting began almost by accident on the morning of September 19, when Thomas sent John Brannan's division, followed by Absalom Baird's, to reconnoiter the Chickamauga. There Brannan's Federals drove back Forrest's cavalry until the Yankees were hit hard by States Rights Gist's division from W. H. T. Walker's Corps. Thomas threw in Baird's division to steady the line until it, too, was beaten back by Walker's other division, under St. John Liddell. The seesaw battle grew furious, but neither side could gain an advantage. "The Chickamauga lived up to its name that day," later wrote Col. Thomas Berry, one of Forrest's officers. "It ran red with blood."

Colonel John T. Wilder commanded the Federal "Lightning Brigade," named for its swift, decisive movements at Stones River. At Chickamauga Creek, Wilder's outnumbered cavalrymen valiantly defended Alexander's Bridge, slowing the advance of William Walker's Confederate corps and buying precious time for the Federal army to consolidate its forces.

ORDER OF BATTLE
ARMY OF THE TENNESSEE
BRAGG
66,300 MEN

RIGHT WING
POLK

POLK'S CORPS

CHEATHAM'S DIVISION

JACKSON'S BRIGADE
MANEY'S BRIGADE
SMITH'S BRIGADE
WRIGHT'S BRIGADE
STRAHL'S BRIGADE

HILL'S CORPS

CLEBURNE'S DIVISION

WOOD'S BRIGADE
L. E. POLK'S BRIGADE
DESHLER'S BRIGADE

BRECKINRIDGE'S DIVISION

HELM'S BRIGADE
ADAMS' BRIGADE
STOVALL'S BRIGADE

WALKER'S CORPS

GIST'S DIVISION

COLQUITT'S BRIGADE
ECTOR'S BRIGADE
WILSON'S BRIGADE

LIDDELL'S DIVISION

GOVAN'S BRIGADE
WALTHALL'S BRIGADE

LEFT WING
LONGSTREET

BUCKNER'S CORPS

STEWART'S DIVISION

BATE'S BRIGADE
CLAYTON'S BRIGADE
BROWN'S BRIGADE

PRESTON'S DIVISION

GRACIE'S BRIGADE
KELLY'S BRIGADE
TRIGG'S BRIGADE

HINDMAN'S DIVISION

ANDERSON'S BRIGADE
DEAS' BRIGADE
MANIGAULT'S BRIGADE

HOOD'S CORPS

KERSHAW'S DIVISION

KERSHAW'S BRIGADE
HUMPHREYS' BRIGADE

JOHNSON'S DIVISION

FULTON'S BRIGADE
GREGG'S BRIGADE
McNAIR'S BRIGADE

LAW'S DIVISION

SHEFFIELD'S BRIGADE
ROBERTSON'S BRIGADE
BENNING'S BRIGADE

CAVALRY

WHEELER'S CORPS

WHARTON'S DIVISION

CREWS' BRIGADE
HARRISON'S BRIGADE

MARTIN'S DIVISION

MORGAN'S BRIGADE
RUSSELL'S BRIGADE
RODDEY'S BRIGADE

FORREST'S CORPS

ARMSTRONG'S DIVISION

J. T. WHEELER'S BRIGADE
DIBRELL'S BRIGADE

PEGRAM'S DIVISION

DAVIDSON'S BRIGADE
SCOTT'S BRIGADE

ARMY OF THE CUMBERLAND
ROSECRANS
58,200 MEN

XIV CORPS THOMAS

FIRST DIVISION: BAIRD
Brigades: SCRIBNER, STARKWEATHER, J. KING

SECOND DIVISION: NEGLEY
Brigades: J. BEATTY, STANLEY, SIRWELL

THIRD DIVISION: BRANNAN
Brigades: CONNELL, CROXTON, VAN DERVEER

FOURTH DIVISION: REYNOLDS
Brigades: WILDER, E. KING, TURCHIN

XX CORPS A. McCOOK

FIRST DIVISION: DAVIS
Brigades: POST, CARLIN, HEG

SECOND DIVISION: JOHNSON
Brigades: WILLICH, DODGE, BALDWIN

THIRD DIVISION: SHERIDAN
Brigades: LYTLE, LAIBOLDT, BRADLEY

XXI CORPS CRITTENDEN

FIRST DIVISION: WOOD
Brigades: BUELL, WAGNER, HARKER

SECOND DIVISION: PALMER
Brigades: CRUFT, HAZEN, GROSE

THIRD DIVISION: VAN CLEVE
Brigades: S. BEATTY, DICK, BARNES

RESERVE CORPS GRANGER

FIRST DIVISION: STEEDMAN
Brigades: WHITAKER, J. MITCHELL

CAVALRY
R. MITCHELL

FIRST DIVISION: E. McCOOK
Brigades: CAMPBELL, RAY, WATKINS

SECOND DIVISION: CROOK
Brigades: MINTY, LONG

General Nathan Bedford Forrest, the Confederate cavalry commander, was a self-taught military strategist whose very simple but effective maxim was "to get there first with the most men." The first shots of the Battle of Chickamauga were fired when John Croxton's brigade of the Federal XIV Corps encountered Forrest's mounted troops and opened fire. After Chickamauga, Forrest had a clash with the fractious Bragg and was transferred.

236

Patrick Cleburne, who emigrated from Ireland at the age of 21, was one of only two foreign-born officers to attain the rank of major general in the Confederate army. Known as the Stonewall Jackson of the West, he led a division of Hill's Corps at Chickamauga.

AFTERNOON ACTION

Through the rest of the day on September 19, the two armies surged back and forth, roughly along the lines shown here. The Confederates launched an attack against Horatio Van Cleve's division, which had marched north to reinforce the Union line. The assault bent back the center of the Federal line, but counterattacks by the divisions of Brannan and James Negley in the center, and Philip Sheridan and Thomas Wood on the right, halted the Confederate advance. Cleburne's division attacked on the Federal left in the late afternoon but was repulsed by the divisions of Richard W. Johnson and Baird. Later that evening, Longstreet, with most of his men, arrived to reinforce Bragg.

Newly arrived from Virginia, troops of Longstreet's 1st Corps detrain at Ringgold, Georgia, to join Bragg's army in the fighting at Chickamauga Creek. "Never before," recorded a staff officer, "were so many troops moved over such worn-out railways. Never before were such crazy cars—passenger, baggage, mail, coal, box, platform—used for hauling such good soldiers."

At twilight on September 19, Cleburne's division surges forward through the woods to attack the Federal line, visible under the trees in the distance. As night fell, troops of both sides had to aim their weapons by sound and muzzle flashes—occasionally firing on their comrades in error.

238

POLK'S ATTACK, SEPTEMBER 20

On the night of September 19, the leaders
of both armies drew up orders for the next
day's battle. Rosecrans opted to assume a
defensive stance, placing Thomas in charge
of the left, McCook the right, with Crittenden in reserve. Bragg meanwhile reorganized his army into two wings, giving
Polk command of the right and Longstreet
the left. Adhering to the original plan of
first assailing the Union left with Polk's
command, Breckinridge's division of Walker's Corps attacked at 9:30 a.m. on September 20, attempting to envelop Thomas'
flank and seize the LaFayette Road. By
10:15 a.m., elements of Negley's and Brannan's divisions had driven back the Rebel
attack. Cleburne attacked next, at about
10:00 a.m., but his men were also
repulsed. At 11:00 a.m., the Federals managed to turn back additional assaults by
two of Liddell's brigades, and later Steedman's two brigades stopped a flanking attempt by Forrest's cavalry. As the fighting
shifted down the Confederate line to
Bragg's center and left, the troops on the
north end of the battlefield traded long-
range fire for the rest of the morning.

Confederates load and fire their rifles in the tangled woodland along Chickamauga Creek. The heavily thicketed terrain, noted a Union officer, made for a "mad, irregular battle, very much resembling guerrilla warfare on a vast scale, in which one army was bushwhacking the other."

Confederate Brig. Gen. Bushrod Johnson led the September 20 attack of Longstreet's wing that sent the Yankees running. He had the capacity in battle, noted a superior, to assess a situation at a glance and to exploit it.

General William Lytle, a popular author and poet turned capable commander, was killed leading a desperate charge against thousands of Confederates at Chickamauga on September 20.

With his arm in a sling from a wound at Gettysburg, Gen. John Bell Hood reels in the saddle as he is struck by a Minié ball while rallying his Texas troops at Chickamauga. Some of his men tenderly bore him to the rear, where his leg was amputated.

LONGSTREET'S ATTACK

At 11:30 a.m., Longstreet's wing moved forward against the Federal right with a juggernaut of 23,000 men from Johnson's, Kershaw's, and Law's divisions. At the same time, Thomas, under heavy attack to the north, was clamoring for reinforcements, and in response, Rosecrans shifted several Federal units, including Wood's division. The reason for this fateful decision is unclear, but apparently Rosecrans believed, in error, that Brannan had either withdrawn or pulled back his right, thus exposing Wood's left flank. When Wood received the order to "close in on Reynolds," the only way he could do so was to withdraw from the line and move to the rear of Brannan. Wood dutifully obeyed the order, leaving a gaping hole in the Union line through which the Confederates poured like a tidal wave. To the south Hindman routed Sheridan and Davis, completing the collapse of the Federal right. Despite Wilder's counterattack against the flank of the Rebel onslaught, nearly half of Rosecrans' command was streaming for the rear.

This small pond behind Rosecrans' headquarters, established at the house of a widow named Eliza Glenn, was one of the only sources of water available to the fighting men in the Federal line. The watering hole was known as Bloody Pond because of the injured horses and wounded soldiers who dragged themselves to it and died while drinking.

This painting of the Battle of Chickamauga captures the critical action on Snodgrass Hill during the afternoon of September 20, 1863. Gesturing from his horse in the middle distance *(center)*, Gen. George Thomas rallies John Brannan's bloodied division against the unceasing assaults of Longstreet's Confederates *(background)*. Only the arrival of James Steedman's reserves *(far right)* averted a Federal rout.

General George Thomas was left in sole command of the battlefield when roughly half of the Union army retreated to Chattanooga. A dispatch later informed Rosecrans that Thomas was "standing like a rock," a fact that earned the doughty corps commander the honorific "Rock of Chickamauga."

SNODGRASS HILL

After the Federal army's center collapsed and its right wing disintegrated, Thomas formed a south-facing defensive line on Snodgrass Hill and along adjacent high ground known as Horseshoe Ridge. Against this line Longstreet threw four divisions—Kershaw's, Hindman's, Bushrod Johnson's, and finally Preston's. All afternoon the troops defending the ridge, and those still holding out on the Federal left, repulsed attack after attack. Critical in checking Johnson's many assaults was the arrival of Steedman's reserve division on Brannan's right flank. On the night of September 20, Thomas disengaged, aided by Sheridan and Davis, who had returned to the field of battle at about 7:00 p.m. The Federals withdrew to Rossville through McFarland's Gap. Bragg, skeptical of reports of a Federal retreat, decided not to pursue.

LOOKOUT MOUNTAIN & MISSIONARY RIDGE

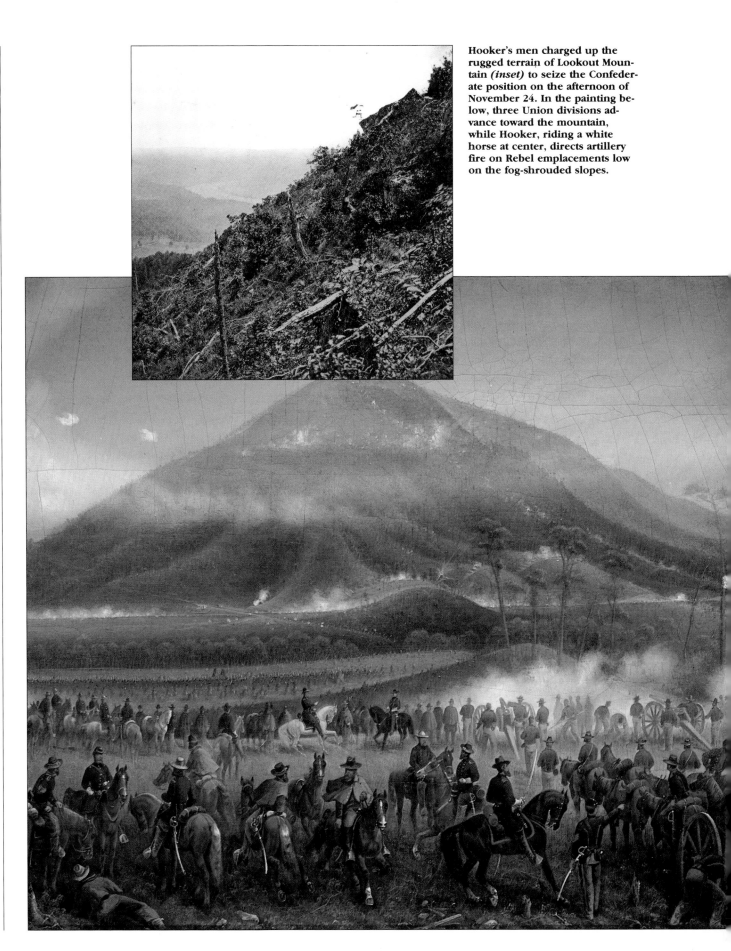

Hooker's men charged up the rugged terrain of Lookout Mountain *(inset)* to seize the Confederate position on the afternoon of November 24. In the painting below, three Union divisions advance toward the mountain, while Hooker, riding a white horse at center, directs artillery fire on Rebel emplacements low on the fog-shrouded slopes.

Following the Union defeat at Chickamauga, Rose-crans withdrew to Chattanooga. Bragg moved up to occupy Missionary Ridge and Lookout Mountain, placing the Federals virtually under siege. In November, Ulysses S. Grant dispatched reinforcements under Hooker and Sherman to launch a three-pronged attack against the Confederates. On November 24, Hooker's forces cleared the Confederates from Lookout Mountain and proceeded to Rossville to threaten Bragg's left and rear. On the 25th, Sherman's troops attacked the Rebel right at Tunnel Hill but were stopped cold by Cleburne's and Stevenson's divisions. That same day, Thomas' divisions under Johnson, Sheridan, Wood, and Baird advanced up Missionary Ridge and routed the Confederate center as Hooker pummeled Bragg's left. The Confederate front dissolved, and Bragg prepared to retreat deep into Georgia.

The Confederate lines of defense are just visible in the distance along the crest of Missionary Ridge. Bragg established three parallel lines of entrenchments—one along the base, one halfway up the slope, and a third along the crest.

Patrick Cleburne's infantrymen and gunners fire into William Sherman's onrushing line at Missionary Ridge. Against overwhelming odds, Cleburne held off the Union force even after the rest of the Confederate defenses on the ridge had crumbled.

Granger, Grant, and Thomas, on a ledge at left, watch from Orchard Knob as their troops swarm up Missionary Ridge in the background. "What was on the summit they knew not," Granger wrote, "and did not inquire. The enemy was before them; to know that was to know sufficient."

Captured Confederate soldiers are held under guard outside Chattanooga's train station as they wait to be sent north to prison camps. According to Grant, more than 6,000 Confederates were taken prisoner in the action at Chattanooga, many during Sheridan's dogged pursuit after the capture of Missionary Ridge.

ATLANTA CAMPAIGN

In March 1864, Ulysses S. Grant, newly named chief of all the Union armies, and his most trusted subordinate, William Tecumseh Sherman, planned a new, coordinated strategy to cripple the Confederacy and win the War. Grant would smash Robert E. Lee's army in Virginia and head for Richmond. At the same time, Sherman would destroy the other main Confederate force, the Army of Tennessee, and seize the key city of Atlanta. Calling itself the Gate City of the South, Atlanta was in fact the strategic back door to the central Confederacy. It was the South's most productive arsenal after Richmond and a critical transportation hub: Four railroads radiating from the city carried supplies to the principal Confederate armies.

Bristling with confidence, Sherman set out from Chattanooga, site of resounding Federal victories the previous November, with no fewer than three armies. The largest was the 60,000-man Army of the Cumberland led by the reliable George Thomas. Smallest was the 14,000-man Army of the Ohio under General John M. Schofield. As his "whiplash," Sherman had his old fast-moving Army of the Tennessee, 24,000 men commanded by the brilliant young James B. McPherson. Facing Sherman were two daunting obstacles. One was the canny Confederate general Joseph E. Johnston with a revitalized army that, when reinforced by General Leonidas Polk's corps, would number more than 60,000 troops. The second was a 120-mile stretch of some of the roughest, most easily defended country in the South—rocky spurs of the Appalachians, swift rivers, and deep valleys murky with dense forest and swamp.

Sherman moved out on May 7, pushing southeast down the Western & Atlantic Railroad with Thomas' army and capturing the critical rail tunnel at Tunnel Hill. Scho-field and Thomas advanced toward Dalton, Georgia, while McPherson marched on a parallel route to the west *(map, right)*. The first significant clash came at Dalton, where the Confederates were dug in on a craggy wall of quartz aptly called Rocky Face Ridge and on hills commanding nearby Mill Creek Gap *(overleaf)*. Sherman attacked, but his movements against Johnston's defenses were merely feints. In a tactic that he would use repeatedly, Sherman sent McPherson and, shortly afterward, the bulk of his army on a wide flanking maneuver that threatened the Confederate rear and forced Johnston to retreat.

Johnston stood again at Resaca, where after sharp clashes on May 14 and 15, he found himself outflanked once more and was forced to withdraw. The pattern was repeated at Allatoona Pass, then at Dallas and the nearby crossroads of New Hope Church. Finally Johnston spread his three corps under Polk, William Hardee, and John Bell Hood along formidable Kennesaw Mountain and its foothills. Here Sherman mounted a frontal assault—and saw his army being chewed to bits. Resorting again to a flanking maneuver, he pried Johnston from the hilltops and at last shoved the Confederates back past Smyrna and across the Chattahoochee River into the outskirts of Atlanta.

There the entire campaign changed character as Johnston, who had retreated 100 miles but had kept his army intact, was replaced by General Hood. Immediately, Sherman found his forces assailed by furious attacks, including Hood's climactic effort at the Battle of Atlanta. But in almost two months of marching and fighting, Hood wore his army out and was obliged to retreat with the survivors south of the city. Sherman had Atlanta and a significant victory in the West for the Union.

WILSON'S CREEK

Courtly, silver-haired Pap Price, leader of Missouri's Confederates, was a prewar governor of the state and a U.S. congressman who had gained military experience leading a volunteer unit that served in the Mexican War. Like many of Missouri's pro-Southerners, Price had migrated west from Virginia with his family in 1831.

Boldly chasing the Confederates into southern Missouri in July 1861, General Lyon suddenly found himself in a perilous position, his army having dwindled to only 6,000 men as many 90-day volunteers decamped for home. The Confederates meanwhile had consolidated General Price's cavalry with Governor Jackson's 7,000 infantry, and they had been reinforced by 4,500 troops from Arkansas led by a tough Texan named Ben McCulloch. Outnumbered, Lyon decided his best hope was a bold attack. Sending a column under Franz Sigel around the right flank of the Confederate camp at Wilson's Creek on the night of August 9, Lyon attacked at dawn the next day with his main force of 3,600, hitting the enemy position on a rise soon known as Bloody Hill. Lyon's troops rolled the surprised Confederates off the hill and soon Sigel's artillery began blasting at the enemy rear. But the Confederates reacted swiftly. Price's men fought savagely for Bloody Hill, and McCulloch's infantry routed Sigel's troops. Soon Lyon, trying to rally his troops, was shot from his horse. Leaderless, the Federals fell back to Springfield and beyond.

Albert Pike *(far left)*, a 300-pound Boston-born scholar and Arkansas planter who knew several Indian languages, was the Confederate representative to the tribes of the Indian Territory—today's Oklahoma—and recruited a force of Cherokees who fought beside the troops of Ben McCulloch *(left)* as part of Van Dorn's army at Pea Ridge. McCulloch, a veteran of the Texas war for independence, had been a Texas Ranger and a Mexican War scout.

His arm in a sling, General Price *(left foreground)* rallies his men as Federals, in the distance, make a final advance at Pea Ridge.

General Samuel R. Curtis, a somber West Pointer and former Iowa congressman, had maneuvered the Confederates back into Arkansas before Van Dorn made his abortive thrust that ended at Pea Ridge. The overall Union strategy called for Curtis to deal with Van Dorn and Price in Missouri while Ulysses S. Grant attacked the Confederates in Tennessee.

On March 6, 1862, Van Dorn found Curtis' Federals deployed atop Pea Ridge, a bluff overlooking the main road to the north. Rejecting a frontal attack, Van Dorn started his command on a night flanking march up Bentonville Detour, a secondary road. But the march was slow, and by morning, only Price's troops were behind the Federals, and they had been detected by Union cavalry at the junction of the Detour and Telegraph Road. McCulloch was late in launching his secondary attack to drive off Federal reserves. Curtis sent Col. Eugene Carr's division to hold off Price, then moved units under Peter Osterhaus, Alexander Asboth, and Jefferson Davis to meet McCulloch. McCulloch attacked first with Albert Pike's Indian troops, driving back Osterhaus. But Davis counterattacked from the east, and when McCulloch was killed, the Rebels abandoned the field. To the east, Price and Van Dorn fared better, driving Carr back onto the slopes; but by evening, the Confederates were low on ammunition. Early on the 8th, Curtis merged his forces and attacked *(inset map)*. Price's troops made a stand on a ridge near Elkhorn Tavern, but a strong Union charge sent the Confederates reeling down Telegraph Road, many not stopping until they were deep into Arkansas.

Texas Confederates wasted no time in protecting the state against a feared
Union invasion from the Southwest, sending a battalion of cavalry across
west Texas and into New Mexico in 1861 and following with an army of
3,500 under a veteran officer, Henry Hopkins Sibley *(right)*. By March
1862, Sibley had taken Tucson, defeated the territory's main Federal garrison, led by Col. Edward Canby, in a clash at Valverde, and captured Albuquerque and Santa Fe. The Federals finally countered by recruiting a regiment of Coloradans who marched south into New Mexico and helped
smash Sibley's overextended army at Glorieta Pass, sending the Confederates on a harrowing retreat back across New Mexico.

GLORIETA

Colonel Edward R. S. Canby, senior Union officer in New Mexico, led the garrison of Fort Craig in the February 20 attack at Valverde on Sibley's Texans as they thrust north along the Rio Grande past the Federal outpost. But the Federals, mostly untrained volunteers, were beaten after a sharp fight and were forced to retreat into the fort.

Having taken Santa Fe, Sibley's Confederates, under the field command of Col. William Scurry, boldly headed northeast to attack the remaining Federal strongpoint at Fort Union. But unknown to Scurry, 900 Colorado volunteers led by Col. John Slough, along with most of Fort Union's garrison, were headed south. On March 26, the two forces collided at Glorieta Pass. On the first day, the Federal van, under Maj. John Chivington, smashed into a detachment of Texans at Apache Canyon, a defile at the western end of the pass, forcing the Confederates back. On March 27, both commanding officers brought up the main bodies of their troops, Scurry moving to Johnson's Ranch, Slough to a ranch owned by a Polish immigrant named Kozlowski. The next day, both forces advanced through the pass—except that Slough detached Chivington with seven companies to take a circuitous route across the mountains to the Confederate rear. The battle at Pigeon's Ranch was a repeat of the first day, both sides hammering at each other until Slough pulled back. But the Federal defeat became a victory when word came that Chivington's men had destroyed Scurry's wagon train at Johnson's Ranch. Without ammunition or supplies, the Confederates retreated to Santa Fe, then fled through Albuquerque into Texas, shattering hopes of conquering the Southwest.

Glorieta Pass

Pecos River

Pigeon's Ranch

SCURRY

SLOUGH

SCURRY

Apache Canyon

SLOUGH

Kozlowski's Ranch

CHIVINGTON

Johnson's Ranch

Confederate Supply Train

0   1   2   3

Scale in Miles

RED RIVER CAMPAIGN

Union troops of Gen. Joseph Mower's division of Andrew Smith's corps storm Fort De Russy near the mouth of the Red River.

The powerful ironclad U.S.S. *Neosho* with its big rotating turret glides warily past an exposed mud flat in the upper Red River.

Ordered to cross Louisiana to Shreveport and seize western Louisiana as a staging area for an invasion of east Texas, Gen. Nathaniel Banks in March 1864 assembled an army of about 30,000. Backed by Adm. David Porter's fleet, Banks launched an advance up the Red River. The Federals began well, brushing aside Confederate cavalry at Yellow Bayou and Mansura. They then took Fort De Russy on March 14, the infantry aided by shelling from Porter's fleet. The way open, Porter and two corps led by Gen. Andrew J. Smith, a veteran of the Army of the Tennessee, moved up the Red to Alexandria and met the rest of Banks' army, which had marched via the Bayou Teche. From Alexandria the combined force advanced in early April to Natchitoches, only four days from Shreveport. There Banks decided to move his army by what seemed the fastest route, an old coach road south of the river. It was a dreadful error: The road was muddy and tortuous and took Banks away from Porter's support. Ahead waited Confederate Gen. Richard Taylor, who at last felt he had enough troops to stand and fight. The result was three encounters starting with a Federal rout at Sabine Crossroads and ending in the Battle of Pleasant Hill *(page 312)*. Stiffening Confederate opposition, failure to link up with a stalled advance from south Arkansas, and the need for Banks to dispatch parts of his force to Sherman's advance on Atlanta, shattered the Union campaign.

Major General Nathaniel P. Banks, who had been soundly thrashed early in the war by Stonewall Jackson in the Shenandoah Valley, later restored some luster to his reputation by taking Port Hudson on the Mississippi and by efficiently running the Union occupation of New Orleans. He argued against the campaign up the Red River, perceiving its difficulties, but was forced to proceed by Halleck in Washington.

CONFEDERATE ATTACK

Beginning the major Red River battles, General Taylor's Confederates surprised and routed Banks' vanguard at Sabine Crossroads on April 8, then hit the Federals again at Pleasant Grove. Banks retreated another 14 miles to Pleasant Hill to regroup, bringing up Gen. Andrew Smith's two veteran corps and forming a line across open land that was anchored on both left and right by tree-clad hills. Taylor immediately pursued and, at 5:00 p.m. on April 9, ordered an attack, sending Thomas Churchill's division of Missouri and Arkansas infantry smashing ahead at the Union left while John Walker's Texas division assaulted the Federal center and Hamilton Bee's cavalry attempted to turn Banks' right. Churchill's troops quickly overwhelmed Col. Lewis Benedict's forward brigade, then charged ahead toward the center of the main Federal line and at the corps of General Smith, hidden on a wooded rise.

FEDERAL COUNTERATTACK

The tide of the battle swiftly turned as Smith's veterans charged out of the woods. Pivoting on James McMillan's brigade, the Federals smashed back Churchill's flank, sending some of his troops fleeing to the rear and driving others into Walker's regiments in the Confederate center. With his attack now hopelessly confused and with casualties piling up—the Confederates had lost 2,600 men in two days—Taylor ordered a general withdrawal. The battle was clearly a victory for the Federals, but the nervous Banks that night ordered an ignominious retreat all the way back down the stagecoach road to the river at Grand Ecore, there to rejoin Porter's gunboats. Porter for his part was determined to extricate his fleet before it was trapped by low waters and shot to pieces by Confederates on the high riverbanks. The two leaders soon abandoned the campaign, retreating down the river and barely saving Porter's boats by getting them over the Alexandria rapids *(opposite)*.

Lieutenant Colonel Joseph Bailey, a brilliant XX Corps engineer, devised an intricate system of dams *(below)* that backed up the Red River, raising its water level and allowing Porter's ships to escape by running the rock-strewn rapids at Alexandria.

As a section of Colonel Bailey's main dam gives way, the gunboat *Lexington* races through the churning break under a full head of steam. By May 13 all of Porter's remaining ships were through the gap and steaming for the Mississippi; by May 20, Banks' retreating army was safe from Confederate pursuit beyond the wide Atchafalaya River. The disastrous campaign had cost the Union more than 8,000 men in all, plus 9 ships and 57 guns.

314

ACKNOWLEDGMENTS

The editors wish to thank the following individuals and institutions for their valuable assistance in the preparation of this volume:

Virginia: Annandale—Homer Babcock. Petersburg—Chris Calkins, Petersburg National Battlefield.

123: From *The Gettysburg Campaign: A Study in Command*, by Edwin B. Coddington, Charles Scribner's Sons, New York, 1968—Library of Congress No. 3538, plate 44. 124: Kean Archives, Philadelphia; map by William L. Hezlep, overlay by Time-Life Books—Library of Congress No. USZC4 1530. 125: Map by William L. Hezlep, overlay by Time-Life Books; Museum of the Confederacy, Richmond, Va., copied by Larry Sherer—Library of Congress. 126, 127: Painting by Rufus Zogbaum, courtesy Minnesota Historical Society, St. Paul, and the State Capitol Building, photographed by Gary Mortenson—painting by Peter F. Rothermel, State Museum of Pennsylvania/Pennsylvania Historical and Museum Commission, photographed by Henry Groskinsky. 128: Map by R. R. Donnelley & Sons Co., Cartographic Services, overlay by Time-Life Books—painting by Edwin Forbes, Library of Congress. 129: Courtesy Don Troiani Collection—sketch by Alfred R. Waud, Library of Congress; Valentine Museum, Richmond, Va. 130: Map by Walter W. Roberts. 131: Map by William L. Hezlep, overlay by Time-Life Books; Library of Congress No. BH834 78—painting by W. G. Browne, courtesy Southern Historical Collection, Manuscripts Department, Wilson Library, University of North Carolina/Chapel Hill, copied by Fred Stipe. 132, 133: Library of Congress No. USZC4 977, inset Kean Archives, Philadelphia. 134: Library of Congress, Nos. B811 700A and B811 700B. 135: Painting by Paul Louvier, West Point Museum Collections, U.S. Military Academy, photographed by Henry Groskinsky—map by R. R. Donnelley & Sons Co., Cartographic Services. 136: Table by Time-Life Books; USAMHI, copied by A. Pierce Bounds. 137: Map by William L. Hezlep. 138: Library of Congress; Valentine Museum, Cook Collection No. 3078, Richmond, Va.—drawing by Edwin Forbes. 139: Painting by Julian Scott, courtesy Robert A. McNeil, photographed by Sharon Deveaux. 140: Map by William L. Hezlep. 141: USAMHI, photographed by A. Pierce Bounds; Library of Congress—drawing by Alfred R. Waud, Library of Congress. 142: Drawing by Edwin Forbes, Library of Congress—USAMHI, copied by A. Pierce Bounds. 143: USAMHI, copied by A. Pierce Bounds—map by R. R. Donnelley & Sons Co., Cartographic Services. 144: USAMHI, copied by A. Pierce Bounds; courtesy Nick Picerno—Library of Congress No. B8184 5037. 145: Valentine Museum, Richmond, Va.—map by Walter W. Roberts. 146: Valentine Museum, Richmond, Va.—map by Walter W. Roberts. 147: Painting by Thure de Thulstrup, Seventh Regiment Fund, Inc., photographed by Al Freni—sketch by Alfred R. Waud, Library of Congress. 148: Library of Congress No. B8171 746—Library of Congress No. B8171 729. 149: The Kunhardt Collection—map by R. R. Donnelley & Sons Co., Cartographic Services. 150: Map by William L. Hezlep. 151: Chicago Historical Society Negative No. ICHi-07869—Frank and Marie-T. Wood Print Collections, Alexandria, Va. 152: Mass./MOLLUS/USAMHI, copied by A. Pierce Bounds. 153: Map by R. R. Donnelley & Sons Co., Cartographic Services. 154: Map by R. R. Donnelley & Sons Co., Cartographic Services, overlay by Time-Life Books. 155: Painting by Benjamin West Clinedinst, Jackson Memorial Hall, Virginia Military Institute, Lexington, Va., photographed by Michael Latil; National Archives Negative No. 111-B-6144—Valentine Museum, Cook Collection No. 2740, Richmond, Va. 156, 157: Painting by Jean-Adolphe Beauce, Museum of the Confederacy, Richmond, Va., photographed by Katherine Wetzel; Valentine Museum, Cook Collection, Richmond, Va.—Library of Congress No. B8172 1820; Washington and Lee University, the University Library

Special Collections, Michael Miley Collection, Lexington, Va. 158: From *Deeds of Valor* (Vol. 1), edited by W. F. Beyer and O. F. Keydel, the Perrien-Keydel Co., Detroit, 1906; Library of Congress No. BH82 3803—Library of Congress No. B817 7803. 159: Map by William L. Hezlep. 160: Frank and Marie-T. Wood Print Collections, Alexandria, Va.; Library of Congress No. B8184 10191—drawing by James E. Taylor, courtesy Western Reserve Historical Society, Cleveland, photographed by Michael McCormick. 161: Map by Walter W. Roberts. 162: From *Battles and Leaders of the Civil War* (Vol. 1), the Century Co., New York, 1884-1887—Department of Cultural Resources, North Carolina Department of Cultural Resources, Division of Archives and History, Museum of History, Raleigh; table by Time-Life Books. 163-164: Maps by Walter W. Roberts and William L. Hezlep. 165: Sketches by James E. Taylor, Western Reserve Historical Society, Cleveland, photographed by Michael McCormick (2); painting by Julian Scott, Vermont State House, Montpelier, photographed by Henry Groskinsky. 166: National Archives Negative No. 111-B-5176. 167: Map by Peter McGinn—Library of Congress No. B8184 10467. 168, 169: Painting by John Ross Key, Museum of the Confederacy, Richmond, Va., photographed by Katherine Wetzel; Museum of the Confederacy, Richmond, Va.—USAMHI, photographed by A. Pierce Bounds; map by R. R. Donnelley & Sons Co., Cartographic Services, overlay by Time-Life Books; USAMHI, copied by A. Pierce Bounds. 170, 171: Painting by Edward Lamson Henry, Addison Gallery of American Art, Phillips Academy, Andover, Mass., photographed by Henry Groskinsky—Mass./MOLLUS/USAMHI, copied by A. Pierce Bounds; map by R. R. Donnelley & Sons Co., Cartographic Services, overlay by Time-Life Books. 172: Painting by André Castaigne, 1892, West Point Museum Collections, U.S. Military Academy, photographed by Henry Groskinsky—Frank and Marie-T. Wood Print Collections, Alexandria, Va. 173: Map by William L. Hezlep. 174: Frank and Marie-T. Wood Print Collections, Alexandria, Va.—painting by Tom Lovell, © the Greenwich Workshop, Inc., Conn. 175: Map by Walter W. Roberts. 176: Map by William L. Hezlep. 177: State Historical Society of Wisconsin; USAMHI, photographed by A. Pierce Bounds—Frank and Marie-T. Wood Print Collections, Alexandria, Va. 178: Frank and Marie-T. Wood Print Collections, Alexandria, Va.—Civil War Library and Museum, Philadelphia. 179: Painting by Sidney King, National Park Service, Petersburg National Battlefield, photographed by Katherine Wetzel—map by William L. Hezlep, overlay by Time-Life Books. 180: Valentine Museum, Richmond, Va.; National Archives Negative No. 111-B-2735—Library of Congress. 181: Map by Walter W. Roberts. 182: Map by William L. Hezlep—© the Detroit Institute of Arts, gift of Dexter M. Ferry, Jr. 183: Painting by William L. Sheppard, Virginia Historical Society, Richmond, Va.; USAMHI, photographed by A. Pierce Bounds—Frank and Marie-T. Wood Print Collections, Alexandria, Va. 184, 185: Gift of Willis M. Rose, 1947-87-18, courtesy Cooper-Hewitt National Museum of Design, Smithsonian Institution/Art Resource, New York, photographed by Ken Pelka; Library of Congress No. B8171 7172—map by William L. Hezlep. 186, 187: Map by William L. Hezlep; Civil War Library and Museum, Philadelphia; USAMHI, photographed by A. Pierce Bounds; courtesy Bill Turner—Frank and Marie-T. Wood Print Collections, Alexandria, Va. 188: Frank and Marie-T. Wood Print Collections, Alexandria, Va.—map by William L. Hezlep. 189: Painting by Tom Lovell, © National Geographic Society—Frank and Marie-T. Wood Print Collections, Alex-

andria, Va. 192, 193: Maps by R. R. Donnelley & Sons Co., Cartographic Services. 194: USAMHI, copied by A. Pierce Bounds—U.S. Naval Academy, Beverly R. Robinson Collection. 195: R. R. Donnelley & Sons Co., Cartographic Services. 196: Map by William W. Roberts, overlay by Time-Life Books. 197: National Archives Negative No. 111-BA1172; table by Time-Life Books—Frank and Marie-T. Wood Print Collections, Alexandria, Va. 198, 199: Courtesy Chris Nelson; H. H. Bennett Studio Foundation—map by William W. Roberts, overlay by Time-Life Books; courtesy the Seventh Regiment Fund, Inc., photographed by Al Freni; courtesy Herb Peck, Jr. 200: Library of Congress No. B8172 2173K; Library of Congress No. B816 2844 Al—map by Walter W. Roberts. 201: Frank and Marie-T. Wood Print Collections, Alexandria, Va.—Chicago Historical Society Negative No. ICHi-08002. 202: Map by Walter W. Roberts—Frank and Marie-T. Wood Print Collections, Alexandria, Va. 203: Library of Congress No. B818 100426—courtesy the Mariners' Museum, Newport News, Va. 204: Map by William W. Roberts, overlay by Time-Life Books. 205: Library of Congress; Frank and Marie-T. Wood Print Collections, Alexandria, Va.—Library of Congress No. B8184 1685. 206: USAMHI, copied by A. Pierce Bounds. 207: Map by R. R. Donnelley & Sons Co., Cartographic Services. 208: Courtesy Brian Pohanka—Library of Congress—USAMHI, copied by A. Pierce Bounds. 209: Portrait Library of Congress. Map by William L. Hezlep, overlay by Time-Life Books. 210: Valentine Museum, Richmond, Va.; Library of Congress No. US 262 14973 13246—table by Time-Life Books. 211: Portrait USAMHI, copied by A. Pierce Bounds. Map by William L. Hezlep. 212: From *Photographic History of the Civil War* (Vol. 10), edited by Francis Trevalyan Miller, the Review of Reviews Co., New York, 1912—map by William L. Hezlep. 213: From *Battles and Leaders of the Civil War* (Vol. 3), the Century Co., New York, 1884-1887 (2). 214: Atwater Kent Museum—map by William L. Hezlep. 215: Library of Congress—from *Battles and Leaders of the Civil War* (Vol. 3), the Century Co., New York, 1884-1887. 216, 217: USAMHI, copied by A. Pierce Bounds; map by R. R. Donnelley & Sons Co., Cartographic Services. 218: From *Battles and Leaders of the Civil War* (Vol. 2), the Century Co., New York, 1884-1887 (2). 219: Map by William W. Roberts, overlay by Time-Life Books. 220, 221: Chicago Historical Society Negative No. ICHi-12748; Frank and Marie-T. Wood Print Collections, Alexandria, Va.—Illinois State Historical Society; map by R. R. Donnelley & Sons Co., Cartographic Services, overlay by Time-Life Books. 222: Painting by Tom Lovell, © the Greenwich Workshop, Inc., Conn.—Frank and Marie-T. Wood Print Collections, Alexandria, Va. 223: Map by William L. Hezlep; Chicago Historical Society Negative No. ICHi-10503—USAMHI, copied by Robert Walch. 224: Map by R. R. Donnelley & Sons Co., Cartographic Services, overlay by Time-Life Books—from *Photographic History of the Civil War* (Vol. 10), edited by Francis Trevalyan Miller, the Review of Reviews Co., New York, 1912; Library of Congress No. BH82 4100. 225: Map by Walter W. Roberts—Frank and Marie-T. Wood Print Collections, Alexandria, Va. 226: USAMHI, copied by Robert Walch—painting by Thure de Thulstrup, courtesy Seventh Regiment Fund, Inc., photographed by Al Freni. 227: Map by Walter W. Roberts. 228, 229: Chicago Historical Society Negative No. ICHi-08022; from *Battles and Leaders of the Civil War* (Vol. 3), the Century Co., New York, 1884-1887—photograph courtesy the Kennedy Galleries, New York. 230: Map by R. R. Donnelley & Sons Co., Cartographic Services, overlay by Time-

Life Books. 231: Courtesy the Historic New Orleans Collection (Acc. No. 1979.130)—USAMHI, copied by A. Pierce Bounds. 233: Maps by R. R. Donnelley & Sons Co., Cartographic Services. 234: Portrait courtesy Seward R. Osborne. Map by R. R. Donnelley & Sons Co., Cartographic Services, overlay by Time-Life Books. 235: Table by Time-Life Books; painting by Nichole Marschall, Tennessee State Museum, Nashville, photographed by Bill LaFevor. 236: Pastel drawing by Sadie Waters, Tennessee State Museum, Nashville, photographed by Bill LaFevor; map by Walter W. Roberts. 237: From *The Mountain Campaigns in Georgia,* by Joseph M. Brown, Matthews, Northrup & Co., Buffalo, N.Y., 1890; painting by Alfred R. Waud, Library of Congress. 238, 239: Map by R. R. Donnelley & Sons Co., Cartographic Services, overlay by Time-Life Books; sketch by Walton Taber, Tennessee State Museum, Nashville, photographed by Bill LaFevor. 240: Valentine Museum, Richmond, Va.; USAMHI, copied by A. Pierce Bounds—sketch by Frank Vizetelly, Houghton Library, Harvard University. 241: Map by R. R. Donnelley & Sons Co., Cartographic Services, overlay by Time-Life Books—from *Battles and Leaders of the Civil War* (Vol. 3), the Century Co., New York, 1884-1887. 242, 243: Library of Congress; map by R. R. Donnelley & Sons Co., Cartographic Services, overlay by Time-Life Books—painting by James Walker, U.S. Army Center for Military History, Washington, D.C., photographed by Larry Sherer. 244, 245: Minnesota Historical Society, St. Paul—U.S. Army Center for Military History, photographed by Larry Sherer; map by R. R. Donnelley & Sons Co., Cartographic Services, overlay by Time-Life Books. 246: USAMHI, copied by A. Pierce Bounds—Library of Congress. 247: Courtesy Seventh Regiment Fund, Inc., photographed by Al Freni—Western Reserve Historical Society, Cleveland. 249: Map by Walter W. Roberts. 250: Library of Congress—Confederate Memorial Association, Washington, D.C., photographed by Larry Sherer; table by Time-Life Books. 251: Library of Congress—drawing by Alfred R. Waud, Library of Congress. 252: Library of Congress—from *Battles and Leaders of the Civil War* (Vol. 4), the Century Co., New York, 1884-1887. 253: Map by R. R. Donnelley & Sons Co., Cartographic Services, overlay by Time-Life Books. 254: Library of Congress (2). 255: Map by R. R. Donnelley & Sons Co., Cartographic Services, overlay by Time-Life Books. 256: From *Battles and Leaders of the Civil War* (Vol. 4), the Century Co., New York, 1884-1887—painting by Thure de Thulstrup, courtesy Seventh Regiment Fund, Inc., photographed by Al Freni. 257: Map by William W. Roberts. 258: USAMHI, copied by A. Pierce Bounds—painting by Thure de Thulstrup, courtesy Seventh Regiment Fund, Inc., photographed by Al Freni. 259: Map by R. R. Donnelley & Sons Co., Cartographic Services. 260: Valentine Museum, Richmond, Va.—map by R. R. Donnelley & Sons Co., Cartographic Services, overlay by Time-Life Books. 261: Special Collections (Orlando Poe Collection), West Point Library, U.S. Military Academy, copied by Henry Groskinsky—drawing by Alfred R. Waud, American Heritage Picture Collection. 262: From *Battles and Leaders of the Civil War* (Vol. 4), the Century Co., New York, 1884-1887—map by Walter W. Roberts. 263: Map by Walter W. Roberts—USAMHI, copied by A. Pierce Bounds. 264, 265: The Atlanta Cyclorama, City of Atlanta, Ga., photographed by Henry Groskinsky (2). 266, 267: Library of Congress No. B8172 3719; from *Photographic History of the Civil War* (Vol. 10), edited by Francis Trevalyan Miller, the Review of Reviews Co., New York, 1912—Chicago Historical Society; map by R. R. Donnelley & Sons Co., Cartographic Services, overlay by Time-Life Books—Frank and Marie-T. Wood Print Collections, Alexandria, Va. 268: Frank and Marie-T. Wood Print Collections, Alexandria, Va.—Special Collections (Orlando Poe Collection), West Point Library, U.S. Military Academy, copied by Henry Groskinsky. 269: Map by Walter W. Roberts. 270: Chicago Historical Society Negative No. ICHi-10739. 271: Map by R. R. Donnelley & Sons Co., Cartographic Services. 272: Map by William L. Hezlep, overlay by Time-Life Books—sketch by Alfred R. Waud, Library of Congress. 273: From *Civil War Times Illustrated* (Vol. 8, No. 1), April 1969, Historical Times, Inc.—Mass./MOLLUS/USAMHI, copied by A. Pierce Bounds. 274: USAMHI, copied by A. Pierce Bounds—Tennessee State Museum, Nashville, photographed by Bill LaFevor. 275: Map by William L. Hezlep, overlay by Time-Life Books. 276: USAMHI, copied by A. Pierce Bounds—Frank and Marie-T. Wood Print Collections, Alexandria, Va. 277: Map by Walter W. Roberts. 278, 279: Library of Congress (2); painting by Howard Pyle, courtesy Minnesota Historical Society, St. Paul, photographed by Gary Mortensen. 280: From *Battles and Leaders of the Civil War* (Vol. 4), the Century Co., New York, 1884-1887. 281: Map by R. R. Donnelley & Sons Co., Cartographic Services—Library of Congress. 282: USAMHI, copied by A. Pierce Bounds—Frank and Marie-T. Wood Print Collections, Alexandria, Va. (2). 283: Map by R. R. Donnelley & Sons Co., Cartographic Services, overlay by Time-Life Books. 284: Frank and Marie-T. Wood Print Collections, Alexandria, Va.—painting by George Peter Alexander Healy, the White House Collection. 285: Map by R. R. Donnelley & Sons Co., Cartographic Services, overlay by Time-Life Books. 286, 287: Map by R. R. Donnelley & Sons Co., Cartographic Services. 288: Map by R. R. Donnelley & Sons Co., Cartographic Services—painting by Alfred R. Waud, courtesy Franklin D. Roosevelt Library, Hyde Park, N.Y. 289: Library of Congress No. B8184 10175—courtesy The New-York Historical Society, New York. 290: The Chrysler Museum, Norfolk, Va.—courtesy Jay P. Altmayer, photographed by Larry Cantrell. 291: Library of Congress—the Mariners' Museum, Newport News, Va.; map by R. R. Donnelley & Sons Co., Cartographic Services. 292: USAMHI, copied by A. Pierce Bounds—map by Walter W. Roberts. 293: Houghton Library, Harvard University—USAMHI, copied by Robert Walch. 294, 295: Painting by Conrad Wise Chapman, Museum of the Confederacy, Richmond, Va., photographed by Larry Sherer—Old Court House Museum, Vicksburg, Miss. 295: South Carolina Historical Society—painting by Conrad Wise Chapman, Museum of the Confederacy, Richmond, Va., photographed by Larry Sherer. 296: Map by Walter W. Roberts; Valentine Museum, Richmond, Va. 297: From *Battles and Leaders of the Civil War* (Vol. 4), the Century Co., New York, 1884-1887—map by R. R. Donnelley & Sons Co., Cartographic Services. 298: National Archives No. 111-B-5889—The New-York Historical Society, New York. 299: Map by R. R. Donnelley & Sons Co., Cartographic Services. 300: USAMHI, copied by A. Pierce Bounds—courtesy Beverly R. Robinson Collection, U.S. Naval Academy. 301-303: Maps by R. R. Donnelley & Sons Co., Cartographic Services. 304: Map by R. R. Donnelley & Sons Co., Cartographic Services, overlay by Time-Life Books. 305: Map by R. R. Donnelley & Sons Co., Cartographic Services, overlay by Time-Life Books—Valentine Museum, Cook Collection 2869, Richmond, Va. 306: Courtesy Dr. Thomas P. Sweeney; Library of Congress—painting by Sgt. Hunt P. Wilson, Museum of the Confederacy, Richmond, Va., photographed by Katherine Wetzel. 307: Maps by Walter W. Roberts (2)—courtesy Dr. William J. Schultz. 308: Map by R. R. Donnelley & Sons Co., Cartographic Services, overlay by Time-Life Books—Library of Congress No. B8172 1976. 309: Library of Congress No. B8172 6574—map by William L. Hezlep, overlay by Time-Life Books. 310: Frank and Marie-T. Wood Print Collections, Alexandria, Va.—Paul De Haan. 311: Courtesy Chris Nelson; map by William L. Hezlep, overlay by Time-Life Books. 312: Maps by Walter W. Roberts. 313: Michael W. Waskul—M. and M. Karolik Collection of American Water Colors and Drawings, 1800-1875, Museum of Fine Arts, Boston.

BIBLIOGRAPHY

BOOKS

Barrett, John G., *Sherman's March through the Carolinas.* Chapel Hill, N.C.: University of North Carolina Press, 1983.

Bigelow, John, Jr., *The Campaign of Chancellorsville.* New Haven, Conn.: Yale University Press, 1910.

Boatner, Mark Mayo, III, *The Civil War Dictionary.* New York: David McKay, 1959.

Borcke, Heros Von, and Justus Scheibert, *The Great Cavalry Battle of Brandy Station.* Winston-Salem, N.C.: Palaemon Press, 1976.

Bowman, John S. (Ed.), *The Civil War Almanac.* New York: World Almanac Publications, 1983.

Castel, Albert, *General Sterling Price and the Civil War in the West.* Baton Rouge, La.: Louisiana State University Press, 1968.

Catton, Bruce:
Grant Moves South. Boston: Little, Brown, 1960.
Never Call Retreat. New York: Pocket Books, 1965.

Chambers, Lenoir, *Stonewall Jackson: The Legend and the Man* (Vol. 1). New York: William Morrow, 1959.

Coddington, Edwin B., *The Gettysburg Campaign.* New York: Charles Scribner's Sons, 1968.

Connelly, Thomas Lawrence:
Army of the Heartland. Baton Rouge, La.: Louisiana State University Press, 1982.
Autumn of Glory. Baton Rouge, La.: Louisiana State University Press, 1971.

Cozzens, Peter, *The Battle of Stones River: No Better Place to Die.* Chicago: University of Illinois Press, 1990.

Crownover, Sims, *The Battle of Franklin.* Franklin, Tenn.: Tennessee Historical Society, 1955.

Dabney, R. L., *Life and Campaigns of Lieut.-Gen. Thomas J. Jackson.* New York: Blelock, 1866.

Daly, R. W., *How the Merrimac Won.* New York: Thomas Y. Crowell, 1957.

Davis, Burke, *Sherman's March.* New York: Random House, 1980.

Davis, George B., Leslie J. Perry, and Joseph W. Kirkley, *The Official Military Atlas of the Civil War.* New York: Fairfax Press, 1978.

Davis, William C. (Ed.), *The Image of War, 1861-1865* (Vols. 1-6). Garden City, N.Y.: Doubleday, 1981.

Downey, Fairfax:
Clash of Cavalry: The Battle of Brandy Station, June 9,

1863. New York: David McKay, 1959.

Storming of the Gateway: Chattanooga, 1863. New York: David McKay, 1960.

The Editors of *Life, Great Battles of the Civil War.* New York: Time Inc., 1961.

The Editors of Time-Life Books, The Civil War series. Alexandria, Va.: Time-Life Books, 1983-1987.

Esposito, Vincent J. (Ed.), *The West Point Atlas of American Wars* (Vol. 1). New York: Frederick A. Praeger, 1967.

Fisher, Leroy H. (Ed.), *Civil War Battles in the West.* Manhattan, Kan.: Sunflower University Press, 1981.

Frank Leslie's The American Soldier in the Civil War: A Pictorial History. New York: Stanley-Bradley Publishing Co., 1895.

Frassanito, William A.:

Antietam: The Photographic Legacy of America's Bloodiest Day. New York: Charles Scribner's Sons, 1978.

Gettysburg: A Journey in Time. New York: Charles Scribner's Sons, 1975.

Freeman, Douglas Southall, *Lee's Lieutenants:*

Vol. 1, *Manassas to Malvern Hill.* New York: Charles Scribner's Sons, 1942.

Vol. 2, *Cedar Mountain to Chancellorsville.* New York: Charles Scribner's Sons, 1943.

Vol. 3, *Gettysburg to Appomattox.* New York: Charles Scribner's Sons, 1944.

Gibbons, Tony, *Warships and Naval Battles of the Civil War.* New York: Gallery Books, 1989.

Glatthaar, Joseph T., *The March to the Sea and Beyond.* New York: New York University Press, 1985.

Gragg, Rod, *Confederate Goliath: The Battle of Fort Fisher.* New York: Harper Collins, 1991.

Henderson, G. F. R., *Stonewall Jackson and the American Civil War* (Vol. 1). New York: Longmans, Green, 1909.

Horn, Stanley F., *The Army of Tennessee.* Norman, Okla.: University of Oklahoma Press, 1952.

Johnson, Robert Underwood, and Clarence Claugh Buel (Eds.), *Battles and Leaders of the Civil War.* 4 vols. New York: The Century Co., 1884-1887.

Lanier, Robert S. (Ed.), *The Photographic History of the Civil War* (Vol. 10). New York: The Review of Reviews Co., 1912.

McDonough, James Lee:

Chattanooga: A Death Grip on the Confederacy. Knoxville, Tenn.: University of Tennessee Press, 1984.

Shiloh: In Hell before Night. Knoxville, Tenn.: University of Tennessee Press, 1980.

Stones River: Bloody Winter in Tennessee. Knoxville, Tenn.: University of Tennessee Press, 1980.

McDonough, James Lee, and Thomas L. Connelly, *Five Tragic Hours: The Battle of Franklin.* Knoxville, Tenn.: University of Tennessee Press, 1983.

McWhiney, Grady, *Braxton Bragg and Confederate Defeat: Field Command* (Vol. 1). New York: Columbia University Press, 1969.

Pfanz, Harry W., *Gettysburg: The Second Day.* Chapel Hill, N.C.: University of North Carolina Press, 1987.

Scaife, William R., *The Campaign for Atlanta.* Atlanta: William R. Scaife, 1985.

Scott, Robert Garth, *Into the Wilderness with the Army of the Potomac.* Bloomington, Ind.: Indiana University Press, 1985.

Sears, Stephen W., *Landscape Turned Red: The Battle of Antietam.* New Haven, Conn.: Ticknor & Fields, 1983.

Stackpole, Edward J., *Chancellorsville: Lee's Greatest Battle.* Harrisburg, Penn.: Stackpole, 1958.

Symonds, Craig L., *Battlefield Atlas of the Civil War.* Baltimore: Nautical and Aviation Publishing Company of America, 1988.

Tanner, Robert G., *Stonewall in the Valley.* Garden City, N.Y.: Doubleday, 1976.

Tucker, Glenn, *Chickamauga: Bloody Battle in the West.* Dayton, Ohio: Press of Morningside Bookshop, 1976.

The War of the Rebellion: A Compilation of the Official Records of the Union and Confederate Armies. Series 1, 2, 3. Washington, D.C.: Government Printing Office, 1889.

Winters, John D., *The Civil War in Louisiana.* Baton Rouge, La.: Louisiana State University Press, 1979.

Wise, Jennings Cropper, *The Long Arm of Lee.* New York: Oxford University Press, 1959.

Zimmermann, Richard J., *Unit Organizations of the American Civil War.* Cambridge, Ontario, Canada: Rafm, 1982.

PERIODICALS

Ballard, Michael, "A Good Time to Pray: The 1864 Siege of Plymouth." *Civil War Times Illustrated,* April 1986.

Castel, Albert, "Victory at Corinth." *Civil War Times Illustrated,* October 1978.

OTHER PUBLICATIONS

National Geographic Society, "Battlefields of the Civil War." Map.

National Park Service:

"Chancellorsville: Part of the Master Plan." Map.

"Gettysburg, First Day, Second Day, Third Day." Maps.

"Troop Movement Map 1: Second Battle of Manassas, August 28, 1862: 5:00 p.m. to 7:00 p.m." Manassas National Battlefield Park, Va. October 1985. Map.

INDEX

Numerals in italics indicate an illustration of the subject mentioned.

A

Adams, John: *274*
Albemarle (ram): *296, 297*
Alexander, E. Porter: 10, 15, 21, 106, *107*
Ames, Adelbert: 301
Anderson, George B.: 80, *83*
Anderson, George T.: 80, 120, 122, 124
Anderson, James P.: 208, 269
Anderson, Richard: 64, 98, 101, 109, 143, *145,* 150, 186
Andrews, John W.: 94
Antietam Campaign: 68-85; *maps* 69, 71, 73, 74, 75, 76, 80, 85
Antietam/Sharpsburg, Battle of: 9, 16, 21, 72-85; *maps* 73, 75, 76, 80, 85; order of battle, 72
Appomattox: 184-189; *maps* 184-185, 188, 191
Archer, James J.: 59, 90, 106
Armistead, Lewis: 49, 131, 132
Asboth, Alexander: 307
Ashby, Turner: 34, 36, 38, *39,* 41
Atlanta, Battle of: 262-265; *maps* 262, 263
Atlanta Campaign: 19, 248-269; *maps* 249,
255, 257, 259, 260, 262, 263, 269; order of battle, 250
Atlantic coast amphibious operations: 288-289; *map* 288
Averell, William W.: 161
Avery, Isaac E.: 128, 129

B

Bailey, Joseph: *313*
Baird, Absalom: 234, 236, 245
Banks, Nathaniel P.: 13, 34, 36, 37, 38, 39, *41,* 56, 57, 59, 230, 231, *311,* 312, 313
Barksdale, William: 125
Barlow, Francis: 9-10, 146, 150
Bartow, Francis S.: 28, *29,* 30, *31*
Bate, William B.: 255, 260, 262, 275, 285
Battery Buchanan: 301
Battery Gregg: 292, 293
Battery Hays: *295*
Battery Robinett: *220,* 221
Beatty, John: 13
Beatty, Samuel: 213, 214
Beauregard, Pierre Gustave Toutant: 24, 25, 26, *27,* 28, 33, *166,* 169, 171, 172, 173, 191, 200, 202, *205,* 206, 296
Bee, Barnard E.: *28,* 30
Bee, Hamilton: 312

Bell, Louis: 301
Benedict, Lewis: 312
Benham, Henry: 292
Benning, Henry L.: 120, 122
Bentonville, Battle of: 280, 281, 284-285; *map* 285
Bermuda Hundred: action at, 167, 168-169; *map* 169
Berry, Thomas: 234
Blair, Francis P.: 269
Blenker, Louis: *32,* 42, *45*
Bowen, John S.: 198, *224,* 225
Brady, Mathew: 19
Bragg, Braxton: *16,* 17, 191, 195, 197, 198, 199, 200, 202, *206,* 207, 208, 211, 213, 214, 232, 234, 235, 236, 237, 238, 243, 245, 246, 285
Branch, Lawrence O'Brien: 59
Brandy Station, Battle of: 112; *map* 112
Brannan, John: 234, 236, 238, 241, 242, 243
Brawner, John: 61
Breckinridge, John C.: 150, 153, 154, *155,* 161, 200, 201, 213, 214, 215, 238
Breese, K. R.: 301
Brockenbrough, John M.: 89, 115
Brooklyn (frigate): 298

Brown, John C.: *266, 267,* 275
Buchanan, Franklin: *291*
Buckland, Ralph P.: 197
Buckner, Simon B.: 208, 234
Buell, Don Carlos: 13, 16, *45,* 191, 195, 200, 203, *205,* 206, 207, 208, 211
Buford, John: 112, 115
Bull Run Campaign, Second: 56-65; *maps* 57, 59, 61, 62, 64, 67
Bull Run/Manassas, First: 7, 20, 24-33; *maps* 25, 26, 28, 30, 33; order of battle, 27
Bull Run/Manassas, Second: 13, 15, 21, 60-67; *maps* 61, 62, 64, 67; order of battle, 60
Burks, Jesse S.: 36
Burnside, Ambrose E.: 16, 19, 21, 26, 28, 29, 69, 73, 85, *86,* 87, 89, 90, 94, 96, 98, 135, 140, 143, 146, 171, 174, 178
Burnt Chimneys, skirmish at: 46
Butler, Benjamin F.: 13, 167, 168, *169,* 219, 301
Butterfield, Daniel: 96, 253

C

Caldwell, John C.: 80, 96, 124
Cameron, James: 7